WRITTEN BY
JOHN HETHERINGTON AND JOHN FORDHAM

ILLUSTRATED BY
JOHN WATSON

A Virgin Book
Published in 1988
by the Paperback Division of
W.H. Allen & Co Plc
44 Hill Street
London W1X 8LB

Typeset by Avocet Marketing Services, Bicester, Oxon
Printed in Great Britain by Cox & Wyman Ltd, Reading

ISBN 0 86369 264 8

This book is dedicated to our families, the dust-covered veterans of our sporadic DIY blitzkriegs. A number of other people also deserve a mention in dispatches for their help on this and other projects. Thanks in particular to Tony Draper for making free with woodworking machinery and tea bags, to Pete Downs for his expert advice, and to John Percival for keeping one member of this partnership out of the casualty ward and the home improvers' wing of the local asylum.

CONTENTS

1

FROM CAVE TO CONCRETE

'Wiv a ladder and some glasses,
You could see to 'Ackney Marshes,
If it wasn't for the 'ouses in between.'
(Edgar Bateman [19th century]:
If It Wasn't for the 'Ouses in Between)

The wide diversity of methods used by *Homo sapiens* (construction division) to keep the rain off is a tribute to the resourcefulness of the species. Through the centuries, almost every available material has been pressed into service on the building-site, and the period between descending from trees and ascending high-rise prefabs has seen countless variations on the theme of Dunroamin. By a cycle of innovation, disaster, correction, adjustment and improvement, a satisfying variety of buildings has emerged that, for the most part, provide permanent shelter and please the eye.

When the earliest des. res. was the cave, Neanderthal estate agents doubtless made a good living pointing out the attractions ('low-level stalactites, very handy situation for the mammoth-trap') but it wasn't long before the young upwardly-mobile hunter-gatherers were opting for the comfort and convenience of thatch-covered holes in the ground and mud huts.

Earth is humankind's oldest building material and it would be quite wrong to despise it. Many examples of cob-walled houses exist in England today in the West Country, Northamptonshire and the Midlands. When there is lime in the earth to harden it, and it is mixed with straw or heather for extra strength, it can be used to construct dwellings that will last for centuries. The usual technique was to build the walls in sections, allowing one to dry out before starting the next, or to raise them inside shuttering of planks or twigs. Limewash and plaster — and sometimes dung — were used to make the walls waterproof, and bullocks' blood was a popular line at the builder's merchants, as it could be mixed into the dirt floor to make it hard and keep down the dust. The smoke went through a hole in the roof — if you were lucky. It was smelly, but it was home.

Five hundred years ago London was built largely of mud. An early example of building regulations aiming to effect improvements was a 1419 edict proclaiming that mud chimney stacks should be pulled down and replaced by stone and brick. Mud continued to be popular stuff, however, even into the 19th century. In 1856 all of Naseby was of mud construction and around the same time a number of settlements rejoiced in the name of Mud Town, a major problem for the postal service.

The strongest cob houses are made from earth containing chalk, and as late as the twenties there was a plan to revive the technique to make homes for ex-servicemen on the edge of Salisbury Plain, one of the best areas for chalk cob. Because cob cottages may at some time have been faced with plaster, cement or even brick, they are not always easy to spot today, but the thickness of the walls — anything up to 1.2 m (4 ft) — rounded corners (which prevent cracking) and thatched roofs are the common indicators.

The fact that stone was laboriously cut by hand until the industrial revolution made it far too valuable for anything except the homes of the wealthy, churches and public buildings. Regular citizens, however, were by the Middle Ages experimenting with timber framing to construct their homes, and for several hundred years this adaptable and simple style dominated domestic architecture. Lengths of timber, usually oak, were jointed and pegged together to provide the shell of the building. Builders even adopted primitive prefabrication, often cutting the timber away from the site and then transporting it. The panels between the framing might have been filled with anything from planks, cob and brick to slabs of rough stone, elm laths and, most famously, wattle and daub — woven hazel twigs coated with a clay that had been mixed with exotic substances such as mutton fat, cow dung, animal hair and flax stems. The plasterer who practised this ancient craft was known to his clients as the 'daubator', a tradesman not easy to locate in today's *Yellow Pages*. In towns, these sometimes rickety buildings became narrower and narrower in response to a tax on the length of street frontage. Builders were legally bound to make sure that the projecting 'jetties' were at least 9 ft above the ground so that a person on horseback could ride underneath, and here we have an example of at least one regulation that modern builders and home improvers are free from.

Where stone was freely available walls had always been constructed of rubble. As methods of stone-cutting improved, quoins were used as corner-stones, and in the prosperous South of England cheap ashlar (cut stone) became commonly used to face all but the poorest buildings. Today the geology of a district will be exposed by the stone of its buildings: flint, limestone, granite, sandstone and slate.

The secret of using heat to convert clay into bricks appears to have been revealed to the ancient Britons by the Romans, but when the invaders left the locals promptly forgot it, possibly after over-indulging on looted wine. It wasn't until Tudor times that brick again became popular — and then only among the wealthy, because it was expensive to use and often had to be transported long distances. Henry VIII and Wolsey built St James's Palace and Hampton Court out of brick, even though they could well have afforded stone, in order to display their affluence and taste for the newfangled. Early bricks are not red but salmon coloured, indicating firing at low temperatures in inefficient kilns. Uneven firing also results in bricks of slightly different sizes or distortions.

The devastation caused by the Great Fire of London in 1666 and an enthusiasm for the classical ideals of the Renaissance combined to produce two new orders of tradesmen, the spec builder and the jerry-builder. The Rebuilding Act of 1667 banned wooden construction, introduced the first building inspectors and standardized a house design that developed into the style known as Georgian. Costing was suddenly made easy for the builder with a pattern book to hand, while the popularity of the style and a growing prosperity, particularly in London, ensured a sale. But with speculative building came bodgery. Walls were not keyed into each other properly, and builders hid the resulting cracks with stucco; wood was placed under brick to make quick foundations, and when this rotted whole buildings moved; floors were so poorly constructed that some leases stated 'there shall be no dances given'. They skimped on the thickness of brick walls, and these economies affected the weatherproofing of the house. The mortar was such poor stuff — mixed with the dust of ground old bricks — that it was sometimes necessary to build fires against a wall to get it to set. Strength was reduced still further by the use of 'bonding' timbers instead of brickwork to tie walls together. In 1735 the architect Isaac Ware spoke out against 'the art of building slightly', complained that many houses would collapse before their lease expired, and added: 'Nay, some have carried the art of building slightly so far that their houses have fallen before they were tenanted.' The Building Act of 1774 went a long way towards outlawing jerry-building by specifying house dimensions and construction in great detail.

By the early 19th century stucco had swept the country as brick went out of fashion. This 'Roman' cement was intended to give the appearance of stone to houses made in less grand materials. The early renderings frequently dropped off as rain penetrated them. Later the more effective Portland cement rendering was used, earning the name 'Portland' from its alleged similarity in appearance to the expensive Portland Bill limestone so popular for prestigious public buildings. Meanwhile, inside the house, plaster and the first mass-produced wallpapers were replacing wooden panelling.

The Victorians' great contribution to housing was the introduction of public health acts and mains drainage, in response to the havoc wrought by cholera and other plagues nurtured in the slums established by rapid industrialization. Enlightened industrialists devised model cottages for their work-forces, and the alarming assertion that ordinary people deserved decent housing led, in the following century, to garden suburbs, progressive estates and semis. Successive regulations dealing with health, construction standards and building dimensions were introduced, shaping the appearance of houses almost as much as the materials used to construct them. One hundred years ago the stairs were the main trunk route for domestic traffic in the form of buckets of coal, pans of ashes, oil for lamps, jugs of water and china bowls of sewage. Slowly the traffic came to a halt as central heating, hot- and cold-water supplies, gas, electricity and indoor WCs became common.

The destruction of cities in the Second World War gave architects of the modern movement the chance to impose their grand vision of machine-age housing. In the thirties they had been restricted to sneering at the enormously popular half-timbered semis of the celebrated 'Bypass Tudor' design and producing flat-roofed, concrete-walled houses with curved steel window frames. Now they were able to move thousands into pre-formed concrete slab and glass towers which were ideologically correct if grim to inhabit.

In 1968 the collapse of Ronan Point in East London following a gas explosion also shook the foundations of official faith in system-building techniques. Vandalism, crime, dirt, shoddy design, bad materials and the despair of young families and old people trapped on the 23rd floor by a wrecked lift finally brought down the whole concept. The architectural principles of the suburbs may be dull, but they work, and the vast majority still hold them dear. New estates, particularly in the private sector, have long since abandoned 'rational' grid layouts in favour of more natural ones, and designers are increasingly ransacking history for elements that will give a brand-new home a comforting touch of the traditional. The progress of bulldozers across post-war Britain and Utopian experiments with concrete have led to an emotional and financial premium being put on the past.

Although houses being constructed today may look similar to much older ones the similarity is not much more than skin deep. Behind the traditional brickwork are to be found improved materials, higher standards of design and a wealth of technological innovation. If you're going to take on either those in the building trade or the vendors of dwellings on an approximation to equal terms, it helps to know how houses got to be the way they are. This is particularly true if, like most of us, you buy a house that's been resisting the elements and the fates for a good many decades. And if you're a 'new-build'-owner, you need to know how houses are being designed and built today. This is covered in the chapter on building techniques, but for now here is a rough guide.

OLD CONSTRUCTION

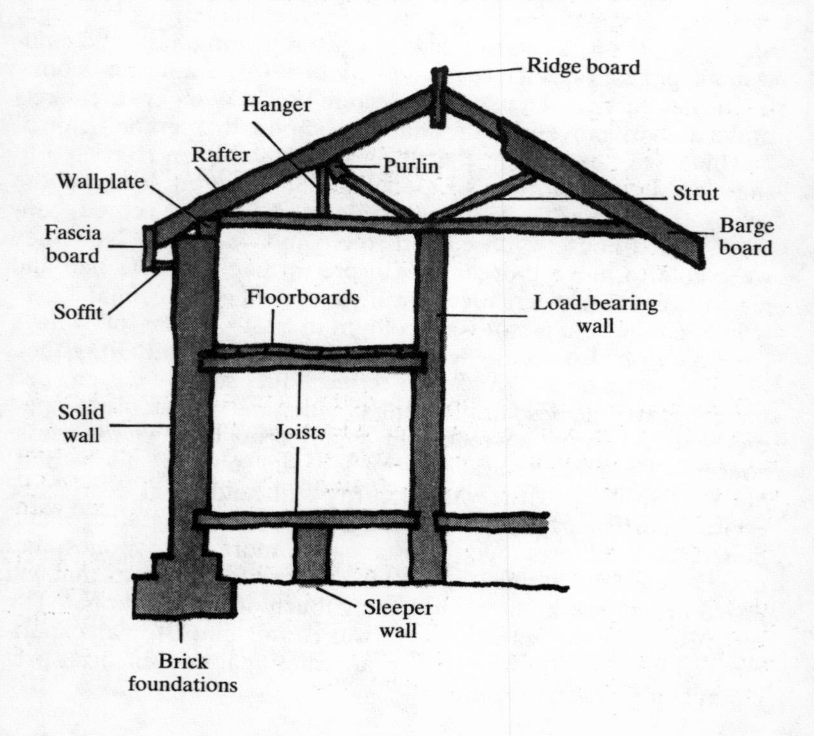

NEW CONSTRUCTION

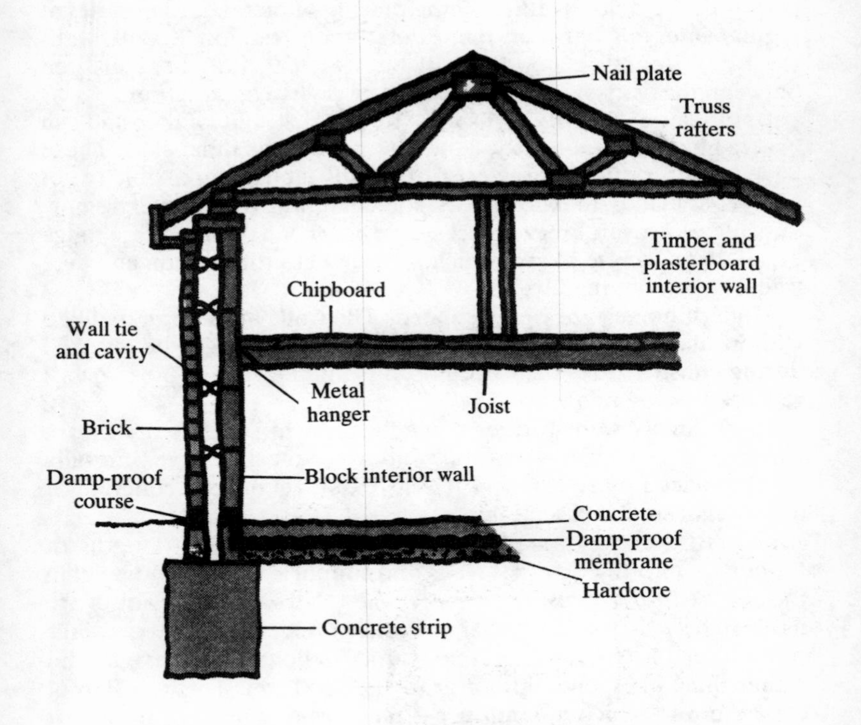

Older houses are invariably provided with **foundations** by a widening of the brick walls below ground level. In modern houses, the walls are usually built on a concrete **strip**, but they can also be erected on a **raft**, a slab of concrete under the whole house, or on concrete columns called **piles**. The concrete may be reinforced with steel mesh or rods.

A **damp-proof course (DPC)**, in which an impervious layer is set low down in the walls to prevent moisture rising through the brickwork, will probably be absent in properties built before the end of the 19th century or even later. Early DPCs of tar and slate have been replaced by rolls of polythene.

Since 1945 all walls have been double-skinned, with a **cavity** that acts as a barrier to the entry of damp and the escape of heat. The two walls are held together by the placing of metal or plastic **ties** at regular intervals between them during construction. Cavity walls are rarely found in houses built before 1919, but those erected between the wars may be either solid or cavity construction.

Both leaves of cavity walls used to be brick, but clinker and ash **breeze blocks** subsequently came into use for the inner skin. These have the infuriating characteristic of being almost impossible to get a screw-hold into, making the attachment of wall furniture extremely difficult. However, breeze blocks have now been replaced by a range of aerated concrete blocks which provide better insulation and take wall fixings more readily.

Modern homes are well **insulated**. The wall cavities can be filled with insulation foam or beads, or insulation board can be inserted during construction. Insulation of lofts and **lagging** of pipework is regarded as essential.

Stone **lintels** were formerly widely used to support brickwork over openings such as doors and windows. Now they have generally been replaced by **rolled-steel joists (RSJs)**, reinforced concrete or lightweight steel box sections.

Floors have traditionally been supported on **joists**, lengths of timber set into the external walls and supported at ground level in the centre of the house by **sleeper walls**. Nowadays the joists are likely to be set into metal brackets, called **hangers**, fixed to the walls or to other joists. However, many modern homes will have a solid rather than a suspended floor at the gound level. This is a slab of concrete into which a **damp-proof membrane (DPM)** of plastic or bituminous material has been inserted. Suspended floors will now usually be covered with sheets of plywood or chipboard that slot together, rather than with the softwood boards that were once common. Suspended floors have the advantage of being warmer but the disadvantage of being susceptible to rot in places that are never seen. Solid floors are cheaper, but harder if you fall on them, and also colder, unless polystyrene insulation board has been sandwiched in the concrete during construction.

Internal walls are no longer made of brick but are either blocks or **stud partitions**, timber framing covered with plasterboard. The lime, sand and horsehair plaster that is still found on the walls of old houses has been superseded by gypsum formulations, and the wooden laths that provided a base for the plaster by **expanded metal lath**, a kind of metal trellis. But today ceilings and walls are less likely to be plastered than to be **dry lined** by having plasterboard fixed against them and then skimmed with plaster or decorated directly.

Roof construction has changed dramatically in recent years. **Flat roofs**, which at one time could be made weatherproof only with sheet lead, are now common, thanks to the introduction of bitumen-coated felts and special plastics. A traditional **pitched roof** is constructed on the site and consists of lines of **rafters** set at intervals and supported by **purlins** running the length of the roof. Where the rafters reach the apex of the triangle they are fixed to a **ridge board**. The bottoms of the rafters rest on the **wallplate** and are tied across the house by the timbers that act as ceiling joists. Purlins are supported by **struts** and joists by **hangers**. This method of construction has largely given way to that of **truss roofs**. These are a series of timber triangles, jointed with toothed metal plates in a factory before being transported to the site, where they are assembled in place. Truss roofs need no support from internal walls and are quick and cheap to install. Their chief disadvantage is that the triangles are so narrowly spaced that the loft becomes an unusable tangle of timber.

Externally, roofs appear to have changed little. The exposed ends of the rafters are still usually hidden by a **fascia board** running along the top of the wall, and the space underneath may be enclosed by a wooden **soffit**. At the gable end, the ends of the purlins and ridge board can be closed off with a **barge board**. Roofs are now **under-felted** with waterproof material to guard against leaks. On top of this go the **battens** to which slates and tiles are fixed. Concrete tiles have superseded clay ones as they resist the weather better. The metal strips called **flashings** in valleys and around chimney breasts were traditionally made from sheet lead, but nowadays zinc and aluminium are common.

Inside the house, cast-iron and lead pipes have been discarded in favour of those made of copper, stainless steel and uPVC. A staggering variety of building boards such as hardboard, chipboard and blockboard has been substituted for solid timber. Doors and window frames are now made from uPVC and aluminium as well as from wood, while heating is controlled by a microchip-operated boiler, radiators and storage heaters rather than by a sooty drudge with a firelighter in one hand and a poker in the other. Internal sanitation, trouble-free drainage and instant access to electricity and gas have all come to be regarded as everyday necessities.

2

A BUYER'S GUIDE

'I wouldn't say the house was small,
but even the rats were round-shouldered.'
(Traditional comedian's patter)

Buying a house, the financial press gravely points out, is the biggest investment the ordinary person will make. The problem is that the ordinary person is not experienced in making large investments and buys too few houses to become an expert at it. In the words of one candid estate agent: 'I sell fifty houses a week. You may buy five in a lifetime. How do you think you can beat me at this game?'

In order to compete successfully in the property market the prospective purchaser needs to have a sharp grasp of financial matters, a profound knowledge of building methods and nerves of high-carbon steel. More usually, these qualities are translated into the financial acumen of a drunken sailor and the observational resources of Blind Pugh. A typical scenario:

The vendor is amiable and apparently honest. The buyer has come prepared with a list of searching questions but is quickly disarmed by a cup of tea, two Bourbons and an affectionate cat. A determination to be businesslike slowly evaporates during a chatty and casual tour of the house. But it is as the buyer is about to leave that the vendor pulls off his master-stroke. With a sudden display of visible unease, he confesses that his conscience will not permit him to let the buyer leave without being made aware of a drip behind a wash-basin that would take six months to fill an eggcup. The house is sold at this point. The buyer is completely won over by this demonstration of scrupulous honesty. Only after moving in does the medieval wiring emerge, the hot-water supply so slow that the bath cools more quickly than it fills, the sieve where the roof should be, the ceilings protected only by buckets and rusty soup-cans strategically deployed in the loft.

Serious house buyers are never caught out in this way. To watch people at work who are completely dedicated to uncovering every cash-draining secret a house may conceal is a daunting but inspiring sight. They turn all the taps on to check the water pressure, they flush the toilet and inspect the flow at the nearest inspection chamber, they tap the walls like condemned men seeking a secret exit from a dungeon, they manically stab the window frames and roof timbers, they jump up and down on the floor to check for rotting joist-ends, they unscrew power sockets to check the age of the wiring concealed behind them, they spend an age in the attic with a powerful torch. They leave exhausted — but under no illusions.

No one should buy a house without having it properly surveyed, and the bank or building society putting up the mortgage money will insist on a professional assessment of the property's merits and faults. However, this does not mean that buyers themselves need not trouble with such matters. You have to start by weeding out the houses that are not worth surveying in the first place because they are too dilapidated or have faults too expensive to repair. A little knowledge is also useful in order to make sense of the surveyor's report and to assess its implications.

FIRST IMPRESSIONS

The location of the property is the first thing to consider. The shortage of building land in the last few years has resulted in estates being thrown up on old tips and marshy ground that at one time would have been regarded as too treacherous. If the estate has been around for a number of years any problems caused by settlement will have become apparent, but in the case of a brand-new house you will have to put your trust in the builder's reputation and guarantee. Try to revisit the area at different times of the week. A quiet retreat on Sunday may by midweek be a high-decibel hell, besieged by juggernauts and jets and smothered in smoke from the fish-products factory.

Always judge a house by the company it keeps. If it is a semi or on an estate, examine the condition of the neighbouring house or houses. If window frames are often replaced and the barge boards rotten then it is likely that those in the property for sale will also be nearing the end of their life. Look for re-roofing jobs and cracks in external walls. If some of the other houses on an estate are having trouble caused by poor workmanship and materials or by settlement due to skimpy foundations, the buyer should closely inspect the property for sale for similar problems.

Before building regulations insisted otherwise, it was common for post-war builders to forget about lintels and to pile the bricks directly on top of the window frames. This invariably leads to cracking and to repointing, which is clearly visible. It also leads to a course of bricks falling on the head of the joiner or builder who comes to replace those windows when they have lived their allotted span. People who replace the wooden frames with plastic double glazing may also find that the weight of bricks bows the frame and jams the windows. A quick look round could reveal these and other defects in a house before the garden gate is opened.

ROOFS

Having gone up the garden path, linger awhile and review the outside. Start by taking a powerful pair of binoculars and studying the roof, and the chimney if there is one. A cracked slate or chimney pot is not a big job to put right. A dilapidated chimney stack, however, is. The mortar of the stack will have been exposed to severe weathering, hot gases and corrosive soot for many years. Check for crumbling mortar and for any bowing or bending. Simply renewing the mortar — **repointing** — is not a catastrophe, but complete reconstruction is costly. Remember that where a stack is shared with the house next door, the owner's permission will be needed if the whole thing has to be rebuilt.

The roof should be straight and square, although some eccentricities are permissible in ancient houses of great 'character', as long as there is no threat to the structure. Terraced houses may be afflicted by **hogging** (although this can also be seen in some semis), a condition in which the roof is described as breaking its back over the party wall that separates one house from another and the tiles tip up above that shared wall. What has usually happened is that the outside walls have settled while the party wall has remained stable. Alternatively, the roofs themselves have sagged.

The **sagging** of roofs, which makes them bow inwards and the ridge line dip, can be caused by the roof timbers being displaced because they are too weak or have rotted. The cause may also be the outward spreading of the outside walls which support the roof. Settlement due to unstable foundations or vibration from heavy traffic might have caused the walls to move at this height, but more frequently the explanation is that the crucial bottom tie timber spanning the roof has failed, putting the whole weight of the roof on to the walls, which, not surprisingly, are bending under the strain.

A plumb-line hanging from the eaves or even just a careful squint along the line of the wall will reveal whether it is true or not. Where there is a serious sag in the roof and a bowed wall, nothing will pull them straight again and reconstruction is the only answer.

Less alarming is a **rippling** roof which has a series of slight concave depressions. This is commonly due to the rafters being too far apart for the load they are carrying, although failed rafters will create the same effect. Check the condition of the flashing, the metal strips around the bottom of chimney breasts and in valleys, and check whether the ridge tiles are properly cemented in place.

If a semi or terrace has obviously been re-roofed, make sure that there is a neat join where it meets next door's roof, particularly if a different kind of tile or slate has been used. Slates are prone to **nail sickness**, a condition in which their retaining nails corrode away, and the only answer is re-roofing. A cheap way of dealing with a dilapidated roof — and one that you often see advertised in glowing terms these days — is to glue an impervious layer of roofing felt over the slates or tiles, or to have a bitumen or plaster layer sprayed on. This is not an ideal solution. Apart from the fact that it drastically alters the appearance of the house, it both makes it difficult to know how serious the original problem with the roof is and cuts ventilation, and when a proper re-roofing job finally does take place it is likely that the appearance of the old slates or tiles will have been irretrievably impaired and you'll have to replace them at great cost.

WALLS

Brick and stonework should be laid straight and be properly pointed with cement in the joints. Cracks should be treated as very worrying unless they are the small ones that can occur when fresh mortar dries. The cause of structural cracking may be the fact that the wall is spreading outwards or that the foundations are settling unevenly or are too small to spread the load of the house evenly over the ground. The general rule is that roughly vertical cracks indicate settlement and roughly horizontal cracks indicate sideways movement. Look carefully for settlement problems where an extension or added-on porch joins the house. Window panes sometimes crack from the corners as they come under pressure and can be an indicator of structural movement. Cracks in walls may have been filled with cement but this is purely decorative and is of no structural benefit.

Clay is susceptible to underground movement particularly during long dry spells. Walls and foundations can also be affected by the vibration of traffic and by the roots of large trees. As a general rule the root system of a tree will spread as far as the branches, so regard that majestic elm or ash with a jaundiced eye. A structural engineer should be called in to assess the significance of a crack and the repair may involve underpinning with concrete, or partial or complete reconstruction.

The bowing of a wall at the bottom is usually the result of

settlement. Bowing in the middle means the wall cannot take the weight of the roof, probably after the first-floor joists have failed. Bowing of the walls and horizontal cracking along the bricks can also be signs that the metal ties holding the outside wall to the internal one are failing. This is usually caused by water getting through and rusting the ties. Where the damage is not too far gone new ties, which are a kind of corrosion-resistant bolt, can be installed by specialist contractors through holes drilled in the walls and then hidden by mortar.

At one time metal bars were passed straight through houses and plates bolted on to the ends to restrain moving walls, and you'll often see them on the exterior walls of buildings today. But this is not regarded as a satisfactory solution. Tie bars can rust, and only those bricks actually covered by the plate will be fully prevented from bulging further. The real cause of the problem that led to the ties being installed should be tracked down and dealt with.

Clues to the causes of cracks and settlement problems can usually be found inside the house. A large gap under the skirtings indicates that the walls have settled taking the floor with them. A large gap under the skirting on one side of the room only probably means that just that wall has settled. Look for a difference in height between the skirtings where they meet at the corner of the room. Where a wall has bowed outwards badly, the edge of the floorboards may become visible in a bedroom. Even slight movement, though, leads to cracking at the edge of the ceiling in the room below. Similar evidence should be found in a bedroom ceiling where a defective roof is pushing the top of the walls outwards.

DAMP AND ROT

Be suspicious where brickwork on an old house has been painted. Old brick can become porous and rainy weather will result in damp plaster inside if there is no inner wall protected by a cavity. Solid walls can be spotted by the regular use of **headers**, bricks placed end-on to tie the wall together. Where such walls become porous, paint will keep the rain out, but apart from presenting an extra maintenance problem it seals moisture into the house preventing the bricks from 'breathing' and in the end causes damp by different means.

A shiny appearance to the bricks may indicate that they have been coated with a waterproofing liquid to prevent damp, and the same objective might have led to the walls being rendered with cement. A rendered or stucco finish should be checked for cracks and tapped where you can reach to ensure that there are no hollows which will cause it to break up. Cracks in stucco may be due to settlement of the wall behind but it is far more likely that the wrong mix was used — damaged sections can easily be cut out and repaired, however. A white powder on new brickwork is probably efflorescence caused by salts working their way out and is quite normal. However, if the brickwork is more than a couple of years old the efflorescence indicates damp.

Look for wall vents and check that they are not blocked. If they are, be prepared to find signs of rot in joists and floorboards. If the damp-proof course is visible ensure that flower beds or piles of rubble don't rise above it and bridge it. Look for cracked gutters and blocked downpipes and gullies. Even if the weather is fine a faulty gutter or downpipe may be revealed by a stain on the wall behind it.

Wooden door and window frames are subject to wet rot which starts work by softening the timber. Check for this by prodding the wood with a penknife, or with a fingernail if the owner is watching. The flat roof above a bay window is a common trouble spot. It is usually lined with lead or roofing felt which is liable to crack and leak, and if this is the case the stains should be visible inside the house. Soil and leaves can also block up the rain-water outlet creating a miniature swimming pool which overflows down the back of the lead into the room beneath or even brings down the ceiling.

Everyone regards as good news the existence of double glazing, efficient central heating, insulation and draughtproofing inside their new home. However, the bad news is that the banishing of draughts reduces ventilation and causes condensation in attics and under floorboards. This is very much appreciated by the various fungi known as wet and dry rot and by boring beetles, and by the firms that repair the mess they leave.

Entertain or infuriate the vendor by jumping up and down near walls and in bay-window areas to discover whether there is flexing caused by joists rotting where they enter the wall. Get out the trusty penknife again and test floorboards, roof timbers and the bottoms of window frames where the condensation runs into the joints. Don't forget the skirting boards, particularly where they are under windows and against an outside wall.

In an old house the ground-floor joists may have been boarded over in the cellar to create a ceiling. In doing this the householder will probably have cut off any flow of air to the wood and encouraged the fungal spores that are constantly present in the air to get to work. It's worth asking to have the boarding removed at strategic points so that you can inspect the condition of the joists, and some agreement over payment for any necessary repairs to the ceiling must be reached. If a structural surveyor is called in the vendor must agree beforehand to such drastic action. But without it the survey misses a vital link.

New floorboards may be nothing more than replacements for ones damaged by being ripped up a number of times to allow electrical and plumbing work to take place. However, they may have been attacked by rot or woodworm. Check neighbouring boards carefully for signs of infestation in case only the very worst boards have been replaced.

Rather than repair a completely rotten floor downstairs it may be easier to replace it with a solid one, but this is still a messy, expensive job. Solid floors of brick, tile or stone slabs were often laid in the kitchens and cellars of old houses. They may appear dry but once they are covered with, say, vinyl or carpets they will draw dampness up from the ground. Solid floors in modern houses will almost certainly have a damp-proof membrane sandwiched in them to keep them dry. Damp in wood block floors will be indicated by the blocks having swollen and lifted in the centre of the room. Check for hollowness underneath the blocks with a nonchalant tap-dance.

It's no secret that a few rolls of wallpaper and a can of silthane gloss can cover up all kinds of problems. Requests to rip off brand-new wallpaper are unlikely to be treated sympathetically by the long-suffering vendor. However, crumbling plaster or plaster that damp has lifted from the wall will, if tapped with the knuckles, be revealed by a hollow sound.

Look for ripples in the paper showing suspicious unevenness underneath. Polystyrene ceiling tiles are often regarded by bodgers as a panacea for terminally ill ceilings. A powdery surface to plaster or bubbling paint and paper indicate damp. Fresh paint won't be able to disguise the puffiness and cracks in wood that is being devoured by rot. Stains on old wallpaper could just be caused by someone throwing a cup of tea at the cat but the explanation is more likely to be damp. If the wall feels dry don't take this as evidence that the damp has been cured. It may show itself only when there is sustained rain, either rising up the wall because of a defective or absent damp-proof course or coming in through aged, unpointed brickwork. Damp patches on bedroom ceilings may return only once or twice a year when heavy rain or snow is driven between the slates of an unfelted roof by wind of just the right direction and force.

PLUMBING

Ask to see the stopcock which will probably be in the kitchen. A **rising main** emerges from this to carry the cold water up to the storage tank in the loft. If this pipe is lead or iron it is likely that the whole plumbing system is antiquated — modern systems use copper. Turn on taps upstairs and down to check that they work and that there is sufficient pressure to give a reasonable delivery, so that you don't have to take a day off work every time you want a bath.

Feeble mains cold-water pressure can be overcome by the installation of a larger or second cold-water storage cistern in the loft. In older houses the problem is much more likely to be that the pipe bringing the water into the house is too small and furred up. The only answer to this is to dig up the pipe and replace it. You can get an idea of whether furring up is likely to be a problem with all the hot-water pipework by sneaking an inspection of the inside of the kettle: if the inside is covered in a hard white deposit there will be a local problem with hard water and the plumbing is likely to be in a similar state. Such snags can be overcome by having a water-softener installed, but if there isn't one it is important that the hot-water cylinder is an **indirect** one which combats furring by having two separate circulations of hot water. If this has lost you, we go into it more fully on page 59.

In unconverted terrace houses and some old semis one water service pipe from the street could be shared by all the houses rather than each having an independent supply. If everybody in the row is having a Saturday night bath, then the last house on the pipeline will probably have to make it Sunday — and if one house has to turn the water off to mend a burst pipe, everybody's water is cut off. If there isn't a direct supply from the mains you should budget for installing one.

Go and have a look outside at the inspection pit for the drains, the lid of which you can lift by prising with a big screwdriver. The insides should ideally be rendered unless the system is a modern plastic one, and branches joining the main channel should be angled in the direction of the flow. While you are there get someone to flush the WC and watch for a nice, healthy flow. This may seem an excessive precaution but the three families we heard of who moved into the first completed houses on a new estate would disagree. They were fine for a week and a half, but then awoke one morning to find sewage in the baths and sinks. The site agent discovered that in the hurry to make the houses habitable no one had made the final connections into the sewer — the soil pipes from the houses came to a dead end and had been back-filling ever since the families moved in.

HEATING

If it is possible, test the heat of the hot water. It is not unknown for people to live for years with a badly designed, badly installed system that never gets better than warm. Inspect the central-heating system. It if uses radiators check that there is no sign of rust on the bottoms or around the valves through which the water enters and leaves. Very old systems may use 1-in steel piping. Modern **small-bore** systems use 15-mm (½-in) copper pipes while **microbore** systems use copper tubing half that size. Have a look at the boiler and make sure you understand what fuel it uses. Gas is convenient and gas boilers need very little servicing. Oil is cheap at the time of writing but the price can change quickly according to who's who in the Gulf. Oil boilers also need an annual service. Solid fuel systems may be hopper-fed or may require you to be constantly lugging coal and ashes around. Underfloor electric heating and old storage heaters are not easily controllable. Aged ducted hot-air systems can be very erratic. Remember that an old heating system will soon have to be replaced at great expense. Open fires may be romantic to sit by but can also be a nuisance to clean and feed. If you plan to open up a disused fireplace be prepared to discover that the flue has perished and needs relining.

WIRING

In old houses the existence of antique wiring is indicated by round-pin plugs and round Bakelite 'toggle' switches mounted on little wooden plinths called **pattresses**. The nature of the wiring will be a guide to its age. The earliest systems used separate stranded wires in steel trunking or conduit. Next came lead-covered cable containing two rubber-covered stranded copper wires, and this was followed by rubber-sheathed cable carrying two insulated cores and an earthing core. PVC-covered cables as used today were introduced in the early 1950s.

Look at the fuse board. The single box common today was preceded by a clumsy series of separate distribution boxes for the different circuits. The main box in this series will have a switch to isolate the whole system. The fuses, which are thin wires that melt and cut off the current if the system is faulty or overloaded, may be contained in porcelain holders on the live and neutral wires, a technique called **double-pole fusing** and long since abandoned. Modern rewirable or cartridge fuses are just connected to the live wire. Many houses now don't have fuses at all but use a series of switches called **miniature circuit breakers**.

Power circuits used to be wired **radially**, in an octopus-like arrangement whereby each cable emerging from the box goes to one extremity of the house. Modern systems use **ring** wiring, in which power cables leave the box, go round all the power sockets and then return. Thus in houses with ring wiring there are two red wires connected to a 30-amp fuse in the fuse box, the one going out and the one coming back. In radial wiring there is only one. Radial wiring is still used for lighting circuits and for appliances like cookers and immersion heaters.

Gleaming modern plastic switches and sockets should not be taken as proof that the house has been rewired. Unscrew a socket and see what sort of cable feeds it, or go up to the attic where the cable will be visible running across the ceiling joists. It is possible that both new and old cable may be used in the circuits so check in several different places.

DIY rewires can also be a hazard and are often revealed by an untidiness that most professionals would not tolerate. Look for sagging wires that aren't properly clipped, cable running across walls and ceilings instead of being hidden, and switches and sockets that are coming loose or are at strange angles on the wall. The electricity board will check wiring if you are worried, or you can employ a good professional to cast an eye over it. Remember that the electricity board will refuse to connect you up after you move in if they don't like the state of your wiring.

LOFTS

A modern trussed roof should be inspected for bending struts, opening joints, rot, and corrosion of the metal plates that hold the struts together. In traditional roofs the first place to look for rot is the **wallplates**, the timbers that sit on top of the walls and take the rafters and ceiling joists. Particularly vulnerable points, these are also the most crucial to the stability of the roof. Being close to the eaves and mounted on cold brick or stone, wallplates are susceptible to damp and rot. As the wood decays it may move on top of the wall under the pressure it carries, or the rafters themselves may slip. The joists also act as ties between opposite walls, holding them fast against the outward push of the roof, and if they rot at the ends and come loose the result is a sagging roof and walls that spread under the weight.

The purlins are the main structural members of the roof so look along them to check that they have not twisted or bent under the pressure they take. Check that the rafters sit straight and square on the purlins, and look along the ridge board to see that it is straight. If the roof has been insulated ensure that the insulation has not been preventing air from getting in under the eaves. If it has, and no ventilators or gable-end air bricks have been installed, start looking for thriving rot. If there is no insulation be prepared to put some in.

NEW HOUSES

Visitors to show houses get bombarded by the tricks of the trade. Woodchip wallpaper and swirly-patterned Artex ceilings are there to disguise the fact that it is hard to get a completely flat finish with modern dry-lining techniques. A spurious sense of 'walking on air' luxury is given by the use of double underlay under the carpet, and in many show houses the doors have been left off to give a sense of space. Keeping the place warm by running the central heating constantly is believed to engender a sense of security and if the lights are on it's probably because the windows are too small. The garden may have a layer of topsoil on or may even be turfed. This is probably to hide the polythene sacks and builders' rubble which has been dumped there for you to find when you start digging the potato bed. The connoisseur of show-house sales techniques is always delighted to find expensive Italian furniture in every room, *Country Life* open on the sofa and Janet Reger's products casually adorning the bed, the unspoken suggestion being that Joan Collins has just popped out to the shops and these mass-produced brick boxes are being snapped up by hedonists with taste. Lavish fittings also help to blind customers to the fact that the ceilings are the strict minimum 2.3 m (7 ft 6 in) high and there are as few power sockets as the firm can get away with.

SUMMING UP

Very few people will have the time or the energy to inspect a house as thoroughly as suggested above. But here's a quick checklist:

- Examine the area and study 'sister' houses for defects that may occur in the one for sale. Use binoculars to examine the roof and walls.
- A sagging or hogged roof means that the timbers have bent or moved, or that the walls supporting them have moved.
- Cracks in brick or stonework indicate that the walls have sunk or are moving sideways. Other evidence for wall movement can usually be found inside the house around skirting boards and the edges of ceilings.
- Damp produces rot. Examine interior and exterior walls, rendering and plasterwork, check for a damp-proof course and look at the condition of gutters and downpipes. Look for further evidence of damp inside. Condensation inside a house can also cause damp and rot problems.
- Wet rot is common in neglected wooden window and door frames. Old joists and roof timbers are vulnerable where they meet walls.
- Old wiring is revealed by round-pin plugs and sockets, distribution boxes on the fuse board and anything other than PVC-sheathed cable.
- Old plumbing is revealed by lead and iron pipes. Look for furring of pipes. Check for a direct and efficient water supply.
- Weigh up the merits and the age of the heating system.

3

THE PROFESSIONALS

'Left Farmerson repairing the door-scraper, but when I came home I found three men working. Farmerson said that in making a fresh hole he had penetrated the gas pipe. He said it was a ridiculous place to put a gas pipe and the man who did it evidently knew nothing about his business.'
(George and Weedon Grossmith [1847–1912 and 1854–1919]: The Diary of a Nobody)

Whether buying, selling, extending, repairing or improving a house, at some stage everyone needs a pro. This chapter is a brief guide to the services available from the host of experts who make houses their business. Naturally, each inflates their own role and reviles all the others. Architects look on builders as mud-encrusted morons and builders see architects as arty-farty pen-pushers. Building inspectors believe builders to be obsessed with cutting corners, and in return are regarded by builders as nit-picking pedants. They all believe that estate agents make a fortune from *their* efforts.

ESTATE AGENTS

It is very difficult to keep out of the clutches of the estate agents if you wish to acquire or dispose of a house. Before the last war this profession provided a form of outdoor relief for impoverished or ineducable sons of gentlefolk who had few qualifications other than rounded vowel sounds. Now it's a high-tech billion-pound service industry. A survey by *Which?* magazine showed that nearly half the people questioned who had used an estate agent had a complaint. The best way to avoid having to complain is to understand exactly what service an agent is offering before the firm acts for you.

The most common complaint levelled against estate agents is about what is euphemistically described as misrepresenting a property. Beauty, of course, is in the eye of the beholder, but it is difficult to accept a room being described as a bedroom when it is too small to contain a single bed, a shed promoted to the status of conservatory, or a row of houses alleged to have 100-ft gardens when they are only one-tenth of that. But descriptions of property in an estate agent's brochure are actually exempt from the requirements of the Trade Descriptions Act. An agent may, however, be liable under the Misrepresentation Act of 1967 if a house is bought on the basis of an entirely misleading claim, and this is why agents protect themselves with disclaimers such as: 'All descriptions and dimensions and other details are given without responsibility and purchasers should not rely on them as statements of fact.' This essentially means that nothing in the brochure should be taken seriously.

Anyone can set up as an estate agent and the service offered therefore varies wildly. Sellers will often be tempted to take on the agent who gives the most optimistic valuation of the property. It may be the case that this firm is the most energetic in the area and regularly gets higher prices than its competitors. However, an exceptionally high valuation may be a ploy to get the job when there is no hope of making a sale at that price. The result is that false hopes are aroused, the house will sit on the market and become 'stale', and when the sellers get restless they will be told they are asking too much and should reduce the price. An agent who advertises widely and has a prominent high-street position is more likely to sell than one who saves cash on premises and publicity. Look for an agent whose turnover indicates that the stock of houses is constantly changing. Check whether the valuation is sensible by making your own estimate after studying the prices of similar houses nearby. Remember that in fast-selling and high-priced areas such as London the quality of the fittings and decoration will have relatively little effect on the price. In areas where there is less demand, new wallpaper in the lounge could make all the difference.

Study all the agent's terms very closely. If the agreement is a sole agency agreement you will not be able to call in another estate agent if your first choice proves slow to sell. However, the firm's commission will usually be comparatively low. A joint sole agency agreement involves two or more agents who must agree on how the commission will be shared in the event of a sale. A multiple agency agreement gives the commission to whichever agent sells. Where competition between agents is fierce, you're likely to find that fees are negotiable. Instead of the fee being based on a percentage of the value of the house, try offering the agent a fixed sum — say, just less than one per cent.

If you give the agent sole selling rights, the firm will get the commission even if the house is sold through your own advertisement or a friend of Aunt Doris. However, once an agency has advertised a property it is going to take a lot of persuading that it wasn't the firm's publicity that assisted the sale to go through. Unless there is a 'no sale, no fee' agreement, the seller may still have to pay the agent even if the property remains unsold. Check who pays for the advertising and brochures and what range of costs is involved, because under the Estate Agents Act the agent must tell the client what the fees are before any agreement is made. Buyers' money, such as deposits, must be held in a separate bank account and interest must be repaid if it comes to over £10. Finally, always remember that as well as estate agents there are local newspapers and magazines, in which sellers may advertise privately.

And you can always make your own 'For Sale' sign, although desperate attention seekers are warned that the planning regulations will restrict the size of the board.

SURVEYORS

At the word 'survey' many house-buyers' eyes glaze over and they automatically assume that once a survey has been done, the property has been thoroughly checked for defects and they are safe. This is not the case, of course; different types of survey have different purposes.

The valuation survey is paid for by the buyer but is used by the building society or bank to decide whether it will advance the cash for the mortgage. Although the surveyor may spot defects that the lender will insist be corrected, this survey gives the buyer no protection. Its real purpose is to tell the building society that the property could be resold for the amount of the loan — and that is often less than the full price.

Buyers seeking an idea of what condition the property is in can opt for a house-buyer's report, which is cheaper than a full structural survey, but is also less comprehensive.

A structural survey provides the buyer with a report on the structure and finishes of the building, outbuildings, fences and walls and even trees if they are close enough to the property potentially to cause damage. The survey will usually include an assessment of water services, drainage and the condition of the hot-water and drainage systems. This survey is worth the extra money if the house is old or its condition suspect, and you can sue if faults are missed. Fees and the extent of the survey should be agreed beforehand. If the surveyor wishes to look under floorboards or remove panelling or plaster the owner's agreement must first be obtained and a deal struck on repairing any damage. The surveyor may find it necessary to call in specialists to report on outbreaks of rot or the state of the foundations and the resulting charges must be discussed. The surveyor should be properly qualified. Look for initials such as FRICS or ARICS after the name.

BUILDERS

Endless grim warnings about ending up in the hands of building-trade cowboys have resulted in a certain amount of paranoia, with people believing that builders are people who vanish for six months after being given £200 for materials. The truth is that the building profession, like any other, has its villains and incompetents but the vast majority of builders are decent folk who try to do a good job. However, when your money and mental health are at stake it is worth going to some trouble to get a builder you can rely on. These are some recommendations:

- Choose a builder who has been recommended by someone whose judgement you trust. Never allow yourself to be talked into having work done by someone who knocks on the door one morning and claims to have spotted a dangerous chimney stack or dilapidated wall.
- Make sure the builder has experience of the kind of work you want done. One who has not graduated past porches and roof repairs may not be the person for that big extension.
- Ask for details of previous work and go and look at it — don't just take the word of the customer over the phone that the job was done well. After paying out many people are loath to admit that the carpentry is shoddy and the brickwork isn't vertical.
- Always try to get the job priced by three different builders and ask for quotations rather than estimates. A quotation is a fixed price and legally binding whereas an estimate is simply a guide and is liable to be amended later. However, a builder will naturally be wary of giving a fixed price where unpredictable problems may occur, such as hitting rock while digging out for a septic tank.

The prices quoted by builders may vary greatly, but this does not necessarily mean that the dearest is an attempt to defraud. Big building firms have much larger overheads than single-operator outfits. A builder who is overwhelmed with work may quote a high price to discourage a customer and one who is facing a financial crisis may cut the rate to get the work. Too cheap a price is as worrying as an excessively high one. The builder who regularly undercuts the competition will probably just as regularly have to cut corners to make the job pay. An instructive case is that of the shop-owner who wanted a dividing wall removed and couldn't resist a quote from two lads that beat everyone else's by half. It wasn't until work began that he discovered why. They demolished the load-bearing wall without supporting the rest of the structure, and just as the building was about to collapse on them they managed to lift into place their equivalent of a rolled-steel joist, a balk of timber of uncertain strength which they had discovered on a tip. The building survived but the upstairs floor acquired an incline you could ski down.

⋆ Check whether builders will do all the work themselves or whether they intend to sub-contract certain areas. It's no good carrying out an in-depth investigation of one firm if a steady stream of strangers then roll up. However, few builders will saddle themselves with tradesmen they know to be unreliable or incompetent.

⋆ Ask to see the builder's insurance certificate. It should cover public liability and all-risks insurance to protect you from legal action should the milkman fall into a trench.

⋆ Many people will, quite reasonably, want to investigate the financial health of the building firm to reassure themselves that it will not go bust in the middle of the job. In return the builder may want to check the creditworthiness of the customer. People with financial problems are known to find petty faults in order to delay or avoid paying. It is understandable that warnings are issued against advancing cash to builders before work is begun. But small firms may not have credit facilities with local suppliers and it is common practice for the customer to provide money for the purchase of materials. However, full payment should never be made in advance, and builders who suggest it should be treated with grave suspicion. On smaller jobs the customer may be offered in return for a cash payment a discount which, by no coincidence whatsoever, comes to 15 per cent — the current rate of VAT. The accuracy of a builder's declarations to the VAT inspector are no concern of the customer's, but there could be problems later with taking action over unsatisfactory work if payment for it never went through the books. However, builders with a good reputation to protect will always wish to make amends where they or their materials have been at fault.

⋆ Get a contract. Where a job of any size is to be undertaken it is important to have a document signed by builder and client specifying in detail the work to be done, the materials to be used, arrangements for payment, guarantees and so on. Even a small extension can cost a great deal of money and a contract protects both sides and prevents misunderstandings and wrangling over who agreed to what. The Building Employers Confederation (BEC) provides ready-made contracts for different types of work and these can be used as they are or amended to provide specific conditions. The BEC also runs a guarantee scheme to cover its members. For one per cent of the contract price, or a minimum £20 fee, work costing from £500 to £25,000 is guaranteed to be finished in the event of the builder going out of business. The Federation of Master Builders also has a warranty scheme based on payment of one per cent of the contract price. This is valid for jobs worth up to £30,000.

One way of cutting the cost of building work, although it won't appeal to everybody, is to act as labourer for the person you employ. Apart from saving a lot of money it is extremely educational, allows the builder to be able constantly to discuss the course the work should take, and does wonders for the cardiovascular system.

ARCHITECTS

The benefit of using an architect is the variety of services they can offer. They can design houses, extensions and alterations with concern for both the technical and the aesthetic results, they'll be aware of current thinking in the local planning office and so will produce designs that are likely to be accepted, they understand the ins and outs of public health requirements, they can supervise the building work and talk to the contractors in their own language. These paragons will have the letters RIBA after their name, indicating that they are members of the Royal Institute of British Architects.

Where you see 'architectural services' being offered you are likely to find an architectural technician who has qualified in the technical aspects of building design but not in the historical and aesthetic ones. The charges are likely to be lower than those of a fully qualified architect for much the same services. Even cheaper will be an architect's draughtsman working in his or her spare time. A draughtsman will produce cheap and efficient designs and drawings for the householder seeking planning permission for additions and alterations.

People living in or near London, Bristol, Manchester, Durham or Glasgow can get expert advice about their project from a Building Centre. The fee for a consultation is charged on an hourly basis.

PLANNERS AND INSPECTORS

The position and design of a building or alterations are controlled by the council's planning department. It is their job, among other things, to prevent people from building corrugated-iron skyscrapers in areas of outstanding natural beauty. Planning permission usually has to be sought for work that alters or adds to existing buildings, but many minor alterations and extensions are allowed automatically. In theory all planning applications are considered by a council committee, but in practice, unless the application is unusual, the councillors will just rubber-stamp the planners' recommendations. Before any major work is done, check whether planning permission is necessary; the rules are quite complicated and can vary according to the area.

The safety of building methods and the type of materials used are controlled by the Building Regulations. The thickness of the walls, the layout of the drains, the design of the floors, the angle at which the roof is pitched, and a multitude of other matters are covered under these 'regs'. There is one set of Building Regulations for England and Wales, while Greater London, Scotland and Ulster each has its own. While anyone interested enough can buy a copy of the regulations, they make baffling reading for non-experts. The local Building Control Officer must be informed about any major work taking place and building inspectors may turn up to check that the regulations are not being infringed. While builders naturally moan when they are told to alter work or do it differently, the inspectors can be very helpful to amateurs and are worth cultivating with cups of tea.

The Wiring Regulations are drawn up by the Institute of Electrical Engineers to make sure work is carried out safely, and in Scotland these regulations are part of the Building Regulations and must be followed. Elsewhere they are not mandatory, but the electricity board has the sanction of being able to refuse to provide a mains supply to a building that doesn't satisfy the standards.

GRANTS

Grants are based on a 'percentage of eligible expense' and some local authorities will be more generous than others in assessing their contribution. Where there is great demand for grants, money will be harder to get.

Grants fall into the following categories:

- Intermediate grants are the only mandatory ones, to which everyone is entitled on demand. All the others are discretionary. Intermediate grants are for putting in amenities like hot- and cold-water systems, baths and WCs in properties built before 3 October 1961. A grant towards necessary repairs carried out at the same time is also available.
- Repair grants pay part of the cost of structural repairs to houses built before 1919. New roofs and floors and repairs to walls and foundations are covered by this grant.
- Improvement grants provide between 50 per cent and 75 per cent of the expense limit on carrying out work on wiring, heating, drainage, insulation, damp-proof courses and so on, although the proportion can be raised to as much as 90 per cent in cases of extreme hardship. The house must have been built before 3 October 1961, and the council will expect the building to have a life of at least another 30 years, be in reasonable repair and have all the standard amenities.
- Special grants are available to provide fire-escapes and basic amenities for people living in flats.
- Insulation grants pay 66 per cent of the cost of insulating the loft and hot-water cylinder and of lagging pipes. This does not apply if the house was built after 1966 or if it already has loft insulation of more than 30 mm (1¼ in) in thickness.
- DHSS repair grants are available to people already receiving benefit whose living accommodation is substandard and is putting their health at risk.
- Homes in conservation areas or those of historical importance may be eligible for various grants from English Heritage as a result of the Government's attempt to encourage urban renewal. The money is available in the form of a subsidy of 40 per cent of the cost of repair programmes of more than £10,000. The availability of such grants has encouraged sellers to raise the price of the property to make a fast buck, but buyers are warned that grants will not be given for work on houses bought at inflated prices.

4

MAKING IMPROVEMENTS

'This ol' house is getting shaky,
This ol' house is getting old
This ol' house lets in the rain
This ol' house lets in the cold.'
(Hit record by Shakin' Stevens)

There comes a time when every householder casts an eye around the ancestral home and decides, with a weary shake of the head, that 'something must be done'. This course of action may be intended to make the property more appealing to buyers or just to make life more comfortable. If there are serious ailments such as leaky pipes, ancient wiring, damp walls and rotting window frames, these should be dealt with first, either by you yourself or by a specialist or a bit of both. The cures for these and the necessary techniques are explained later. This chapter is more concerned with suggestions for how you can raise the standard of your accommodation without having to apply for a second mortgage or acquire advanced building skills.

DECORATING

Paper and paint are the cheapest means of transforming a house and today's range of textures, finishes and techniques is vast. Life was simple when people painted their walls with distemper and the woodwork with gloss and colours were a self-explanatory light blue or pale green. The modern paint manufacturer is a cross between a chemical engineer and Wordsworth. The emulsions that took over from distemper have now themselves largely been superseded by tougher and more wipable vinyl-based and latex paints, while oil-based gloss has been toughened with polyurethane and alkyds. Meanwhile these complex products are mystifyingly christened 'moon shadow', 'satin romance', and so on. We can't explain the names but here is a guide to the products:

PAINTING

Raw wood, metal, brick and concrete must be **primed** if they are to be painted. The primer prevents paint from being absorbed by the surface, helps to stop stains or marks showing through the finishing coat and provides a good key for the paint that follows. Red lead primers for use on metal and the pink lead-based wood primers are now frowned upon on health grounds. Metal should be primed with a zinc chromate-based product. If rust is present it should be removed with a wire brush and then the metal painted with a primer that converts the remaining rust into harmless magnetite.

Ordinary white primer should be used on softwoods, once they have been sanded and any holes or cracks filled, but highly-resinous wood and hardwoods need treatment with an aluminium wood primer. **Knotting** is a shellac-based varnish used to stop resin bleeding out of knots and to help prevent the knot from showing through the paint. New cement, concrete and brick will need an application of an alkali-resistant primer before being painted. Plasterboard and hardboard can be treated with specialist primers, but thinned emulsion paint will serve well enough. There are also universal primers which will treat wood, metal and plaster quite adequately unless there is a particular problem.

★ **Inside:** The quickest way to cover a wall is with **emulsion** and a roller. A matt finish is best where the surface is imperfect as glossier paints will highlight every fault. The semi-gloss finish, usually called silk, can withstand the occasional wipe down and is good for kitchens and bathrooms and for homes with young children who, for reasons psychiatrists have yet to explain, are unable to pass a wall without wiping a grimy hand across it. Emulsion can now be bought in a non-drip form in its own tray, all ready for the roller, which makes life very easy for the novice.

Oil-based gloss paint can contain alkyd resins or polyurethane. **Alkyd** paints are glossier and survive outdoors slightly better than polyurethane ones. **Polyurethane** dries more quickly, however. Non-drip polyurethane paint is a jelly that becomes liquid only as it is brushed on. It won't drip down your arm, but the drawbacks are that you need more of it to cover the same surface area and it is tricky to use in tight spots such as mouldings and window frames.

Irregular walls can be disguised to an extent by painting techniques such as **sponging** or **rag-rolling**. These also look good applied to tatty furniture. For sponging, use natural sponge plus two, or possibly three, toning emulsion paints in matt or vinyl finishes. Paint the wall with the base colour and then cut the sponge to provide a flat surface. Put the next colour in a dish and dip in the sponge. Dab off any surplus paint on to a piece of paper until a nice speckled pattern is achieved, and then start on the wall. Keep dabbing until the pattern grows faint and then recharge the sponge. If the speckling is too strong in places it can be muted by responging with more of the base colour.

For rag-rolling, use oil-based eggshell colours. First paint the wall with the base colour. Then thin the top colour with an equal quantity of white spirit. Once the base coat is dry, apply the glazing coat. Roll clean cotton fabric into a sausage and, wearing rubber gloves, roll it up and down the wall while the glazing coat is still wet. The glaze is not fast-drying, but if the surface to be covered is a large one it helps to have someone applying this coat in strips while the rolling takes place. As the rag gets soaked in paint refold it to get a clean area on the outside of the roll, and when it is completely saturated replace it. The art is to keep going until the whole wall is finished, so practise first and make sure sufficient materials are to hand. The wall can be finished with a glaze coat of clear matt varnish.

⋆ **Outside**: Life outside the house is tough for paints. Gloss paint on exterior woodwork has a life of only a few years because as the wood expands and contracts, the paint cracks and moisture gets underneath, making it bubble. **Microporous** paint is claimed to be the answer to this problem. It is a water-based paint containing acrylic resin that is flexible and 'breathes', allowing water vapour to pass through it rather than build up a mini-reservoir underneath. It must be used on fresh wood only, and many brands have their own undercoat and primer.

Cement-based paint such as Snowcem comes as a powder that has to be mixed with water. The rough-texture finish lasts from four to seven years. It cannot be used over other paints and must be applied with a roller or synthetic-filament brush, as cement is death to real bristle.

Masonry paints contain fibres or particles of stone, sand or granite which help them disguise small cracks. The life expectancy is about the same as for cement paint.

Specialist-applied coatings are even rougher in texture and should last for 10 years if the surface is properly prepared. Some coatings are less effective than others, and there have also been complaints that some have been damaged by birds pecking at the bits in them. Don't have a wall coated until the company you are planning to hire has given you the addresses of jobs done at least a year or two ago, and you have been to look at them to see how they have fared.

⋆ **Special jobs:** There are specialist paints for every situation. Anti-condensation paint is worth trying in kitchens and bathrooms where the problem is not too serious. It works by acting as a layer of insulation, and some types have particles of absorbent material such as clay or vermiculite. Bituminous paint is used for gutters, water-tanks, walls and wherever there is a need for a waterproof layer. Textured paint such as Artex is used to give a raised pattern by means of a scraper or patterned roller. Fire-retardant paint will help resist flames — unlike gloss, which is highly inflammable — and heat-resistant paint is used where it will be subjected to very high temperatures, such as on the flue-pipe of a boiler. Other heat-resistant paints are designed for exposure to lower temperatures, such as on radiators. Floor paint contains epoxy resin to withstand hard wear, while anti-mould paint contains a fungicide.

STAINS AND VARNISH

Wood stains are an alternative to paint and either come with a built-in varnish or need a compatible one applied on top. They usually come in shades of brown, but red and green are also available for the more adventurous. Don't take the manufacturer's colour-chart too seriously — the final tone will depend entirely on the colour and density of the wood being stained.

⋆ **Inside:** Shellac or French polish and beeswax finishes are fine for furniture buffs but most people will go for a varnish that is alkyd- or polyurethane-based. These varnishes are hard-wearing, heat-resistant and water-repellent and come in both gloss and matt finishes. A sealing coat should be applied first; this should be diluted with white spirit, 10 per cent for softwoods and 25 per cent for hardwoods. Then you can apply thin top coats, making sure the surface is rubbed down between each coat to fill the grain and remove dust and fluff that may have floated on to it while it was still tacky.

Thin coats of matt applied with a cloth and buffed gently with fine-gauge wire wool before waxing will give furniture a dull lustre that resembles the effect of French polish. A quicker and equally good finish can be obtained by using melamine, although this is generally available only from trade suppliers, in 5-litre cans. The advantage is that, like shellac, it dries almost instantly so that a number of thin coats can be applied and rubbed down in a short space of time.

⋆ **Outside:** Yacht varnish is usually recommended for outdoor use but many believe it survives no longer than a conventional polyurethane- or alkyd-based varnish. Like many paints, varnishes are now also microporous, which should prevent bubbling and flaking, and they may be formulated to resist ultraviolet light and mould. They are sold clear or containing a wood-colour stain. An alternative to varnishes are oil-stain preservatives, which are painted on in the same way and offer similar protection. Teak oil gives good protection on the exterior of hardwood window frames and helps preserve the natural finish.

Before we leave the subject of paint and varnish, remember that emulsion paint can be cleaned from brushes with water. Gloss and varnish will need to be removed with white spirit, but the brush will stay soft overnight if immersed in a jar of water. Don't forget it, though, or the brush will soon be stiff enough to hammer nails with. Paint stripper can sometimes resuscitate sadly-neglected bristles.

WALLPAPER

Most papers are machine-printed. The cheaper **pulps** have the design printed directly on the paper, but the more expensive ones are coloured first. **Hand-printed** papers are for those who want something more exclusive and don't mind paying for it, while **relief** papers are good for covering poor surfaces. The cheapest of these is woodchip, which contains bits of wood and sawdust. Anaglypta has two layers of paper embossed with a low-relief pattern, while Supaglypta has a high-relief pattern. There is also Vinylglypta and Foamed Vinyl, which have high-relief patterns and are washable.

Ordinary papers are made washable by having a thin plastic coating put on by the manufacturer. **Vinyl** papers can actually be scrubbed, which makes them ideal for kitchens and children's rooms. **Flock** paper is made by having silk, nylon or wool cuttings glued to the surface. Its success was largely based on its being used to supply oriental restaurants and down-market pubs, but even they now seem to have abandoned it. **Foamed polyethylene** such as Novamura is a textured lightweight plastic material which can be wiped. It is applied by pasting the wall rather than the paper. Apart from plastics, a number of other materials are sold on a paper backing to make them hangable. These include cork, hessian, grasscloth and silk. Ordinary machine-made paper is the easiest to hang, and the job is made simpler still if you use those that are pre-pasted. Instead of adhesive being applied on a table with a brush, these papers are pulled through a trough of water. Relief and fabric papers can stretch when wet and their weight alone makes them more difficult to hang.

Most wall-coverings come in rolls 10.05 m (33 ft) long and 53 cm (21 in) wide. To work out how many rolls are needed to paper a room, first calculate how many strips will be needed by dividing the combined width of the walls by 53 cm. Then calculate how many strips you will get per roll by measuring the height from skirting to ceiling, adding 100 mm (4 in) to allow for wastage, and divide into 10.05 m. If the pattern is a large one, extra rolls may be needed so take this into account in your calculations. Alternatively, forget the whole business, take the measurements of the room to the shop and get them to work it out. When buying, make sure all the rolls have the same batch number or there may be variation in the shade of the colour.

PREPARATION

Surfaces must be properly prepared before painting, papering or varnishing. Skimping on this is tempting when you want to see the final effect, but it will lead to poor adhesion and a lot of hard work wasted. Where old paint is sound it will simply need washing with a mild detergent solution and rinsing. Gloss and varnish should be rubbed down with fine sandpaper to give a key to the new coat, and all the dust should be wiped off with a damp cloth or one wetted with white spirit. If the new paint is a similar in colour to the old, an undercoat will probably be unnecessary. Where there is flaking, all loose paint or varnish must be scraped or stripped off. The edges of the sound paint should be feathered down with abrasive paper and the exposed wood primed.

The hard way to get old paint or varnish off is to sand it. This method has the added disadvantage that where paint is very old and lead-based, a toxic powder is created. It is much quicker and easier to use a gas-cylinder blowlamp. Heat the paint till it starts to bubble and then strip it off with a scraper or shave-hook. The flame must be kept moving or the wood will scorch and window glass will crack. If stripping indoors, have a tray to catch the smouldering fragments of paint and keep a bucket of water handy. A hot-air gun will do the same job much more safely.

Chemical strippers work out more expensive than a blowlamp. They either come as a liquid or are the peel-off type, whereby a strip is stuck to the surface and then pulled off with the old paint attached. The chemicals are nasty to work with, and gloves, old clothes and even goggles are a good idea.

Walls and ceilings textured with a plaster-like compound are a problem if you can't bear to live with them any longer. Plastering over the surface or installing a suspended ceiling is the expensive option. The others are cheaper, but tough on the arm muscles. Powder-based finishes such as Artex will need to be softened with a steam stripper and then scraped off. What is left must be sanded smooth. Washable and paint-like finishes can be scraped off after a special chemical stripper has been applied. On non-washable textured surfaces use paint stripper to get the paint off and then soak the compound until it can be scraped off.

Yellowing or stained polystyrene ceiling tiles must not be covered with gloss paint or the flame retardant finish will be made useless. The tiles can be prised off easily with a scraper but the adhesive left behind may be more difficult to shift. Scraping and sandpapering is the answer, but the ceiling may be left in such a state that a texture finish or embossed paper is required to disguise it.

Cracks are best filled with resin fillers that are mixed with water. They dry hard and smooth and don't shrink. This means they can be applied flush with the surface, unlike cellulose fillers, which need to be applied protruding slightly above the surface and then rubbed down when hard. Damaged render or plaster will have to be cut back to where it is sound and then made good with the appropriate material. Metal should be filled with resin car body filler. For large gaps around pipes, between the skirting board and the wall and round door and window frames, use an expanding foam filler. The semi-rigid finish can be sanded, painted or plastered.

If old wallpaper is smooth and shows no sign of coming loose, paper over it. If it has got to come off, soak it with water to which has been added a proprietory stripper and then scrape it off with a stripping knife. Washable and painted papers will have to be scored first to let the water get through to the pasted surface underneath. In the case of vinyl papers, the face can be pulled off in strips and if the underlayer is sound it can be left on as a form of lining paper. If it isn't sound, then soak it and strip it off. Where the job is a big one it may be worth hiring a steam stripping machine.

Some plasters will have to be left for weeks before they can be papered but other types are usable almost immediately. New plaster and plasterboard should be treated with a primer or sealant before decorating, while old plaster should have a coat of size (weak glue) applied. This stops the wall absorbing water from the paste too quickly and so prevents the paper from dropping off for lack of adhesive. Where emulsion paint is flaking it must be stripped if paper is to be hung over it, but where it is sound a washing-down is all that is necessary. Gloss surfaces need to be rubbed with sandpaper to provide a key.

Painted walls should first be lined, as should irregular walls and those that are to receive heavy papers. Lining papers come in various grades. Medium is ideal for a wall with small cracks. Linen-backed lining paper should be used where the wall surface is breaking up or liable to movement. Extra-white lining paper is best where the surface is to be painted rather than papered. Lining papers should be hung horizontally, against the direction of the paper that goes on top.

FLOORS

Battered, splintered and missing floorboards can be patched up and covered with hardboard to provide a surface suitable for a floor-covering. But if they are too bad for that, rip them up and replace them with tongue-and-groove flooring chipboard. Squeaky boards can usually be remedied with a few extra nails, but keep close to the edges where the original nails are rather than hammering in the middle or you may hit a pipe. Use oval-head nails that can be punched into the wood. Where floorboards are springy rather than just loose the problem is likely to be a rotten or broken joist, and this is where you get a builder in. An expert opinion will be needed on whether to splice or replace a joist, and on whether the condition of the others is such that you may find yourself inspecting the foundations if you tread too heavily. Hollows in irregular solid floors can be filled with a self-levelling compound that is mixed with water and poured on.

Where the boards are in good condition they can, if you want, be sanded. All the nails should be punched below the surface and the cracks filled. Shredded newspaper mixed with wallpaper paste makes a good papier mâché for filling the gaps between the boards, but is tedious to apply. Sealant from a gun is quicker to use, but is expensive and unlikely to match the colour of the stained boards. Stained wood-filler is both expensive *and* tedious to apply, but does the best job. Sanding a floor is not a job to tackle with a block of wood and sandpaper. A drum sander and an edger, the appropriately-named machine for doing the edges where the drum sander won't reach, can be easily hired. The hire shop will also supply assorted grades of abrasive paper for the job.

Before starting, seal the room by fixing masking tape round the doors, otherwise a thick layer of extremely fine dust will coat everything in the house as you create something akin to a storm in the Sahara. The sanders are very powerful and have to be used with some delicacy or they will dig substantial holes in the wood. Switch the machine on, lower it gently to the floor, keep it moving slowly to avoid digging in and switch it off at the end of every run before turning round. Work through the grades of paper from rough to fine, and constantly cross the floor in different directions to avoid creating paths and deepening any grooves that may have occurred. Finish with stain and flooring grade polyurethane varnish, which can be matt or glossy. One of the problems with varnishing is that it catches the light and shows up imperfections that previously were invisible. Perfectionists are recommended to apply a layer of varnish before returning the sander so that any glaring irregularities can be rubbed out.

Woodblock or parquet floors are sanded in the same way as boards. High-quality blocks in timbers like oak and maple can be bought second-hand from an architectural salvage yard for the price per yard of an average-quality carpet. However, to the purchase price must be added the often substantial cost of laying the new floor. Parquet must be laid on a smooth surface and old floorboards are best replaced with chipboard. The blocks are set in a mastic and to avoid cutting them at the edges of the floor, remove the skirting, cut a section off the bottom and replace it over the laid blocks. Modern parquet can be bought in self-adhesive squares which are much easier to handle although lighter weight and often less attractive.

The simplest way to cover a floor that's an eyesore is with carpet or vinyl. Bottom-of-the-range synthetic carpets made of materials such as acrylic and polypropylene are cheaper than decent underlay and are tough as well, although they don't keep their looks. Bargain-hunters should watch out for high-quality wool or wool/nylon mix carpets that are ends of rolls or old lines or have been used for an exhibition. Vinyl has taken over from linoleum, once a feature of every kitchen, and vinyl tiles are much easier to handle than the sheet form. Beware of using printed vinyl where it will get heavy use — the pattern will eventually show signs of wear.

Cork floor tiles are warm, and are tougher than they look. They can be bought ready-sealed or you can finish them yourself with matt or gloss varnish. Proper sealing is essential if they are to be used in the bathroom. Textured rubber used to be available only for contract furnishing but it is now making its way into the domestic market. It is very tough and the non-slip surface makes it ideal where there are very young or old people about.

SHELVES

Shelves are an easy way to rationalise clutter. The simplest we've seen are just planks supported by bricks and they look better than you might think. At the other end of the scale are elaborate built-in units that require skilled carpentry. Single shelves can be held on 'L' brackets fixed to the wall, but an adjustable track system is best for a run of shelves.

If the track is fitted at the back of the shelves it will use cantilever brackets to hold the weight, whereas track fixed at the ends of the shelves will support them on little plugs or metal tags. If the load is to be heavy the two methods can be used in combination. The degree of support a shelf will need depends on what material it is made from: softwood 25 mm (1 in) thick should span 1 metre (39 in) without sagging, but chipboard 20 mm (¾ in) thick will need support every 500 mm (20 in) and 20-mm (¾-in) plywood every 800 mm (31 in). Blockboard must be cut so that the core strips run parallel to the edge of the shelf. Blockboard, chipboard and plywood can be bought with a hardwood veneer. If used in their raw state they can be painted or stained and the front edge lipped with solid wood.

The only difficulty with the track is fixing it to the wall so that filling the shelves doesn't create an avalanche. If the wall is plaster on brick, drill a hole with a masonry bit straight through the plaster and insert a plastic plug to hold the screw. A block wall will need a cellular wall plug.

Expanding plugs, gravity and spring toggles can be used to fix things to hollow stud-partition walls, but neither they nor the plasterboard walls are designed to take much weight. If the shelves are to carry anything more than a few ornaments the screws will have to go into the part of the wooden frame behind the plasterboard. You can usually find this by tapping gently and marking where the hollow sound stops.

KITCHENS

Fitted-kitchen salesmen apparently find it an easy matter to separate their customers from quite astonishing amounts of money in return for chipboard cupboards. However, it is not necessary to spend a fortune in order to have a smart and convenient spot to grill a sausage.

The first thing to consider is whether a new fitted kitchen is needed at all. Old units may be scruffy but the carcasses may be sound enough, so hold on to those you have or offer to provide a home for some being thrown out in an expensive kitchen rip-out. If the units don't quite fit your kitchen plan it is simple to get additional ones that match for they are all based on standard dimensions. You should be able to overcome any disparity in height or depth by adjusting the plinth at the bottom.

Repaint the doors or, for a dearer but more professional finish, persuade the local car body shop to spray them. Alternatively just replace the doors. You can either buy them independently or get a joiner to knock some up. Some firms specialize in making hardwood doors to measure and this still works out cheaper than replacing the whole unit. If the worktop is to be replaced, plastic laminate is tough and cheap and comes in a tremendous variety of finishes. The thickness can be 30 mm (1⅛ in) or a 'luxurious' 40 mm (1½ in). Avoid cheap worktops that have a laminate on the top face only, because they are very likely to warp. Worktops can also be made using plywood or blockboard covered with Formica or tiles for an extremely durable surface. Old mahogany bar counters can often be found in architectural salvage yards and make very impressive worktops once they are stripped and revarnished with polyurethane.

If you are going to buy a completely new kitchen, the cheapest are self-assembly ones that come in a flat pack. Like most units they are based on chipboard faced with white melamine, and the bottom-of-the-range cupboards use board 15-16 mm (⅝ in) thick and have open backs. They come with all the fittings and screws needed together with instructions, and the store selling them will almost certainly help you design the layout and give you tips on installation. Buying flat packs direct from the manufacturer can also be very economical. The hard part is screwing them all together, and it is worth buying or borrowing a cordless electric screwdriver for the job.

Plumbing in sinks and wiring up cookers is well within the range of the do-it-yourselfer who has researched the subject (see Chapters Five and Six), but gas appliances must be installed by a professional. Even they are known to come unstuck, however. One salesman tells how the proud owner of a new kitchen turned on the gas hob for the first time and was drenched with water. It transpired that the fitting team had managed to connect the water to the cooker and the gas to the dish-washer.

BATHROOMS

Old houses are sometimes found to contain bathrooms that appear to be modelled on the engine-room of the *Bismarck*, with massive, wheezing plumbing and chipped enamel baths sporting curious stains. Transforming a bathroom of this type is not cheap, but it is not necessary to install a jacuzzi and sauna in order to make the place habitable.

The bathrooms market is extremely competitive and big stores are always offering special deals. Acrylic and glass-reinforced-plastic (GRP) suites are cheapest and are warm to the touch. Ceramic and enamelled suites are dearer and colder, but last longer. The range of taps and other fittings is enormous but watch our for cheap foreign taps that don't match British plumbing.

A shower uses only about one-fifth of the hot water a bath will take. The simplest and cheapest installation is a combined bath/shower mixer tap, although the spray will lack power compared with that of an independent shower. Tiled walls are practical and look good, but paint is cheaper and quicker. Matt or vinyl silk emulsion should be used, but not gloss as it attracts condensation. Vinyl or cork tiles make a warm, comfortable floor-covering, or you can use carpet with a waterproof rubber backing.

Bathrooms need to be warm to combat condensation as well as for comfort. If central heating isn't available, in a small bathroom use a combined light and heater unit or a heated towel-rail (bigger bathrooms may need a wall-mounted fan heater). *Never* use a plug-in heater. If you have an antique enamelled cast-iron bath it may be worth having it re-enamelled rather than scrapping it, as these are now regarded as the Rolls Royce of tubs. The original enamel would have been heat-fused on to the metal, but the application can now be done chemically on site by specialist firms and prices are very reasonable.

STAIRS

Extra space in a hall can be gained by removing the cupboard under the stairs. This is usually just a stud-and-plasterboard or lath-and-plaster wall which should come out without any difficulty. Destructive rather than constructive talents are required. Rudimentary woodwork skills (see Chapter 7) are only needed if the **newel post** or upright piece holding the banister at the top of the stairs continues down to the hall floor and becomes part of the cupboard structure. If this is the case it will have to be sawn off level with or just below the **string**, the side-piece running from top to bottom into which the ends of the stairs are slotted. The newel post should already be firmly attached to a joist under the landing floor, but if further support is deemed necessary you or a builder can add a metal bracket or drill two 18-mm (¾-in) holes through the bottom of the newel post and joist to take glued wooden dowels. To finish off the job the underneath of the stairs will have to be covered with a **soffit**. Run battens down each side and nail on thin plywood, hardboard or plasterboard, or use timber cladding (see page 50).

STAIR REPAIRS

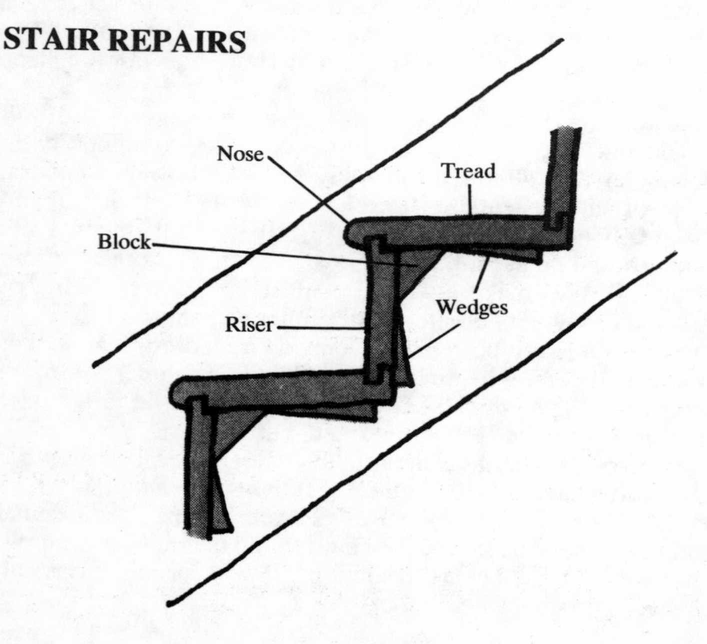

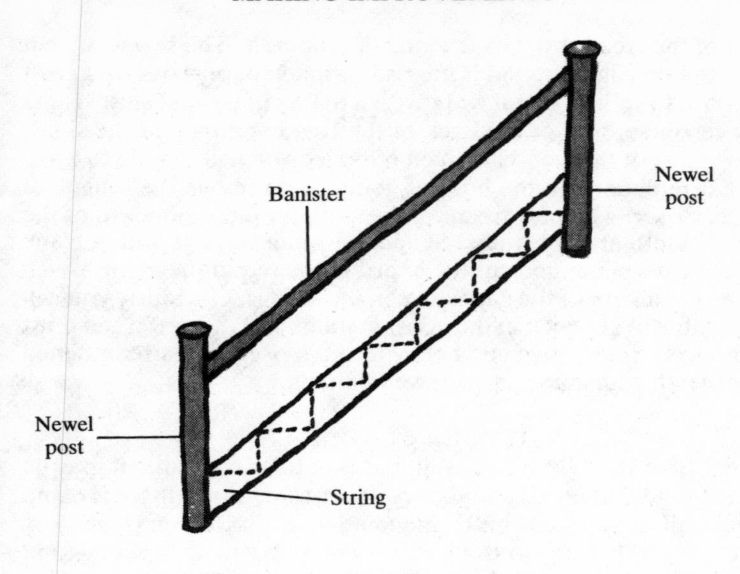

Squeaky stairs are caused by the joints becoming loose as a result of shrinkage and wear. The **treads** of the staircase are the (aptly named) pieces we tread on, and the **risers** are the vertical bits. They are held together by tongued joints. If one of these becomes loose, sink a couple of screws through the tread into the riser to hold them together. Other faults require the underneath of the staircase to be exposed. One possibility is that the problem stair is flexing because the triangular glue-block supporting it has dropped off. Scrape all the old glue off the block, re-glue and screw it back in, after first drilling holes through it to take the screws. The ends of the treads and risers are usually fixed by wedges where they slot into the strings. A loose wedge should be cleaned, given a coating of glue and driven back into the housing joint with a mallet. Damaged or missing blocks and wedges will have to be replaced.

A wrecked or rotten tread will have to be replaced. Use a tenon-saw or padsaw to cut through the tongue of the riser that holds the front of the tread, by sawing along the top of it. The saw won't cut into the housing joint and if the riser is made of plywood you can't rely on it to split. Careful work with a mallet and small chisel is the only recourse. Saw at the back of the tread and then at the sides. When most of the wood has been removed you will be able to clean up that remaining in the housing joints and remove the tongue of the rear riser. The new tread can be simply a piece of board of the correct width and thickness. Shape the rounded nose with a plane and abrasive paper and cut the board to the required length, which will be the length of the gap between the strings. Obviously you will not be able to get back in the housing joints and the new tread must be screwed from above and below into the risers and strengthened underneath with glued and screwed battens.

TIMBER CLADDING

Rather than struggle with a wall that is in poor condition it may be easier to hide it behind a timber cover or **cladding**. If there is damp in the wall, make sure this is remedied first. Fix 38-mm (1½-in) by 25-mm (1-in) battens to the wall with masonry nails or screws and plugs. They should be 400-500 mm (16-20 in) apart if you are using 9-mm- (⅜-in)-thick pine or mahogany boards. Vertical cladding will need horizontal battens and vice versa. Bits of plywood or hardboard may need to be placed behind the battens at certain points so that they form a completely flat surface. Check by laying a long, straight-edged piece of wood across all the battens and make sure none is too high or too low. The tongue-and-groove cladding boards should be fixed by secret nailing, with pins driven through the tongues at an angle into the batten. The head of each pin is

TIMBER CLADDING FOR WALLS

Basic fixing techniques

FIXING THE BOARDS

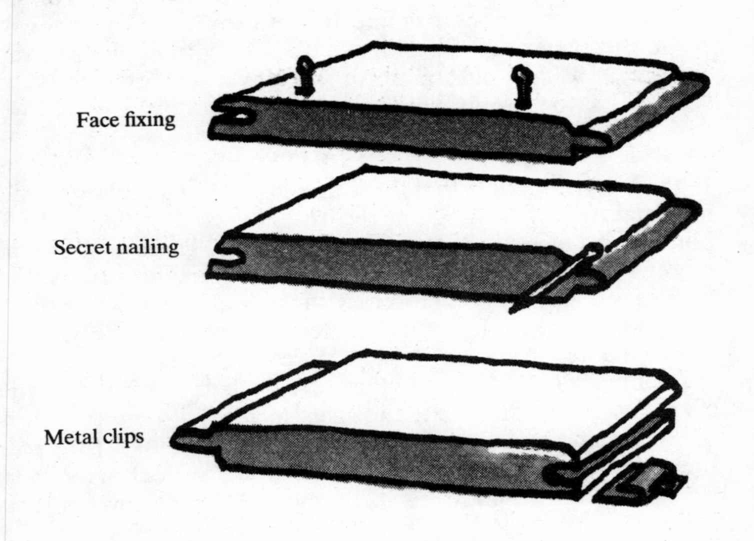

hidden when the groove of the next board is pushed over it. Another neat method uses patent clips. Finish by staining, if you wish, and varnishing.

CEILINGS

Cladding is also one way of dealing with an unsightly ceiling. A range of suspended-ceiling systems is also available for lowering a high room and improving the lighting and insulation. Suspended ceilings are usually supported on a framework screwed to the walls at the desired height and are an efficient way of hiding holes, pipes, stains and electric wiring. Cracks where the wall meets the ceiling can be hidden under moulded coving or plaster friezes. Stick-on centre-pieces and cornices copied from Victorian designs will give a ceiling a stately air, especially if they are picked out in a different colour. Use dark colours on a gloomy high ceiling to make it appear lower, and continue the paint down to the picture rail if there is one.

Light colours should be used on a low ceiling to make it look higher. Remove the picture rail in small rooms and use mirrors and vertically striped wallpaper to create an illusion of more space. Textured paint and paper are the old stand-bys for disguising an irregular surface. If using emulsion make sure any stains are painted with a sealant first to prevent them from showing through.

SECURITY

In the light of the fact that there are more than a million burglaries in Britain every year, good security is both a selling point for a house and a reassurance to the householder. There is no stopping a criminal who is utterly determined to break into a house, but Raffles is unlikely to join forces with the Mafia in order to knock off your video. The truth is that 90 per cent of break-ins are opportunist crimes where advantage is taken of weak security.

Door chains will prevent callers forcing their way in, and a **viewer**, a lens that is set in the door and gives an angle of view of at least 160 degrees, will give you the chance to weigh them up before opening the door. **Rim locks** like the common basic Yale lock are vulnerable to a bit of plastic or a firm kick, as every TV cop show instructs us, and should be replaced with the **deadlatch** version, in which a bar locks into the staple to prevent forcing. Even stronger are **mortise deadlocks**, in which the lock is mounted *in* the door instead of on its surface. From here you can move steadily towards a domestic version of Fort Knox, with deadlocks with anti-saw rollers, steel box striker plates to resist jemmies and hinge bolts that slot into the opposite side of the door to prevent the hinges from being smashed off. One version is surface-mounted on the door and frame and sends bolts into the door frame *and* the floor when the key is turned.

Having given up on the door the prowler next looks at the windows. These can be protected with bars, grilles and roller shutters, but most houses will just want locks operated by keys or number combinations. Make glass doors safe by using laminated glass in them. This has a layer of plastic sandwiched in the middle and is very difficult to break. There is a range of lights with timer devices which will switch on and off while you are out to give the impression that someone is in the house. If you want to get really fancy, curtains can even be drawn at a pre-set time by an electric motor.

If you have a lot of valuables your insurance company may insist you get a burglar alarm. This will have to be professionally installed and regularly inspected. However, DIY alarm kits are available from a couple of hundred pounds. **Wired** systems are linked to a siren or bell which goes off if someone opens a door or window. Pressure pads which detect the presence of an intruder can be put under carpets in strategic spots and linked into the system. **Wireless** systems are similar but use radio waves rather than electric wire to link the detectors to the alarm. **Movement detectors** sense intruders when they break an ultrasonic beam or when their heat is detected by an infra-red sensor. The simplest system is one of individual **door alarms** which require no central control and are set by a key or code.

Free advice on home security can be obtained from the crime-prevention officer at your local police station.

HELP FOR THE DISABLED

The average home can be a frustrating obstacle course for the many people who suffer from a physical handicap. The designers of public buildings are increasingly making provisions for this section of the community but a private home often has to be modified if a disabled person is to live in it safely and independently.

In the kitchen, gas and electric appliances can be fitted with a variety of special knobs that can be manipulated by people with hand disabilities. Worktops, sinks and cookers should be 800 mm (2 ft 7 in) high for wheelchair-bound cooks instead of the usual 900 mm (3 ft). Sinks are available with flexible plumbing so that they can be raised and lowered. Single-lever mixer taps are easier to use than conventional ones and there are even automatic mixer taps with their own temperature-controller. These operate when they sense hands placed under them.

Baths should be shorter than usual with a seat at one end to aid getting in or out. Alternatively, a mechanical lift can be used. Taps should be of the single-lever kind. A shower can be fitted with a seat and controls operated with the knee. WCs should have grab handles, and door locks may need to be versions that can be opened in an emergency from outside.

Stairs can be equipped with handrails on both sides for people who have difficulty walking, or a stairlift can be installed — basically just a folding seat running up a track on the side of the stair.

Wheelchairs need a width of at least 770 mm (2 ft 6 in) to get through doors, and outside the house steps should be replaced by ramps. Paths should be smooth and at least 1 metre (3 ft 3 in) wide. No incline should be steeper that 1 in 12. To save a handicapped person struggling to open the door to a caller, an electric lock and door phone can be installed. Further specialist advice and suggestions can be obtained from disabled people's organisations.

5

PLUMBING, DRAINS AND GUTTERS

'Many of the poor who have no cisterns to allow the water to rest in carry the fluid to be used for washing and scouring from the canals and are frequently so economic in their use of it that they keep the bucketful until it stinks.'
(The Morning Chronicle, *1849*)

The accusation 'You couldn't change a tap washer' is a form of abuse frequently encountered by novice plumbers. The truth is that while technological advance has made many areas of life incomprehensible it has had the opposite effect with plumbing. Modern materials and joints mean that repairs and improvements can be readily launched into by the home handyperson, once the manner in which water wends its way about the house is understood. Learning the fundamentals is helpful. While re-creating the majestic beauty of the Niagara Falls in the privacy of your own home may be impressive it is certainly not desirable.

THE COLD-WATER SYSTEM

Water is supplied to every street by means of a pipe called a **main** which is buried under the road or pavement. The maintenance of this pipe is the responsibility of the local water authority. Each house is connected to the main by a **service pipe**, and when this pipe enters the house it becomes the **rising main**.

INDIRECT COLD-WATER SYSTEM

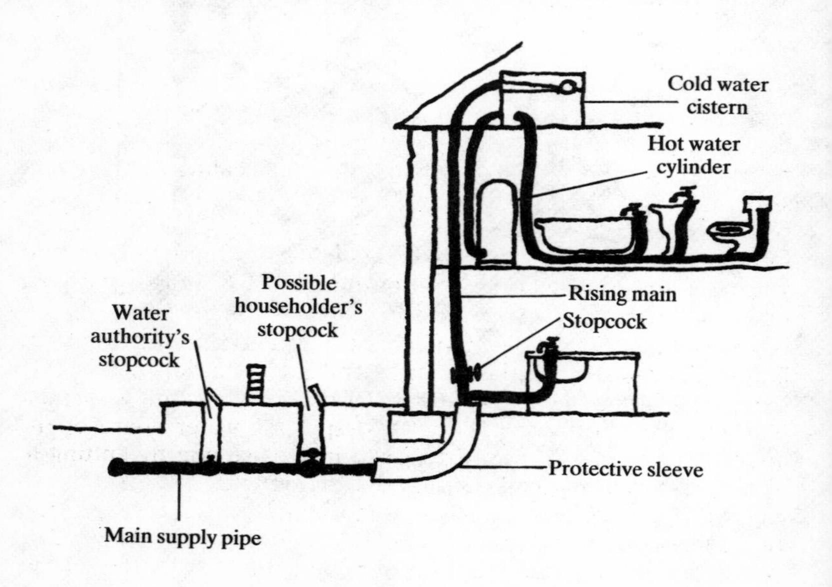

DIRECT COLD-WATER SYSTEM

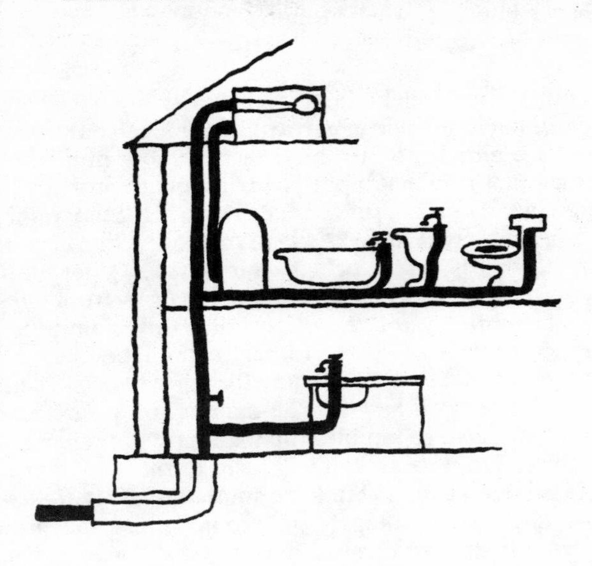

If you want to cut off the water supply you must turn off a kind of tap called a **stopcock**. The water authority will provide a stopcock near where the service pipe joins the main. Stopcock sleuths should be looking for a small hinged metal plate concealing a three-foot shaft, probably sited on the pavement. The stopcock may have a square head instead of the usual handle. This is to stop it being interfered with by bored children, passing vandals and the like, but you may find that it also stops you interfering with it when you desperately need to.

The prudent householder will check out the site of the stopcock before any catastrophe should strike and acquire a stopcock key, a long rod that fits the square section of the stopcock and is carried like a badge of office by every self-respecting water board operative. However, it is also possible to improvise one by cutting a V-shaped slot in the end of a piece of timber and nailing another piece of wood across at the other end to create a handle. There may be a second stopcock in another purpose-built hole in the garden and this is the householder's responsibility. But for all practical purposes the stopcock that is invariably used to cut off the supply is the one in the house. It will be found where the service pipe enters the house — in a cellar close to the street or beneath the kitchen sink.

It is essential for every home to be able to isolate itself from the water supply. In old property, particularly in 19th-century terraces, a single service pipe is often shared by a number of houses. Each dwelling then taps into that pipe. The consequent problems are not hard to imagine. If one household needs to turn off the water supply to allow plumbing work to take place then everyone else must do without water until that work is completed. Other difficulties include loss of pressure when several houses draw from the service pipe at the same time, and the effects of a furred-up pipe in one house restricting the supply to another. An independent supply is therefore a good idea, and the cost and the amount of work involved in getting it depends on how far the main is from the house. The water board will have to tap into the main and provide a stopcock for themselves. From there you will have to run a pipe in a tough but flexible material called **alkathene** some three feet (750-900 mm or 30-36 in say the Building Regulations) under the ground to protect it from frost, and this will have to be shielded in a piece of larger-diameter piping where it goes through or under the foundations.

There are two systems for ferrying cold water from the stopcock throughout the house, direct and indirect supplies:

Direct supply: In this system the rising main goes up through the house with branch pipes leading to the cold taps on wash-basins, sinks and baths and to the WC. The main finally comes to a halt at the top of the house, usually in the attic, where it fills the water-storage cistern that provides the supply for the hot-water system.

Indirect supply: In this system only the kitchen tap is supplied directly from the main so that pure water is available for drinking and cooking. All the other cold-water taps and appliances in the house are fed from the storage cistern along with the hot-water supply.

The indirect system is invariably used in modern houses while the direct is common in older property. It's easy enough to check what system you are dealing with. Close the stopcock on the rising main and turn on the cold taps. If the system is indirect the kitchen tap will dry up within seconds while the others work normally. If the direct system is in use all the cold taps will cease to work.

Some older houses have managed to combine direct and indirect systems as a result of piecemeal improvements to the plumbing over the years. As a result it might be found that the WC draws water directly from the main while the taps are fed from the storage cistern. There is no reason why this shouldn't work well although the occasional Heath-Robinson nightmare does come to light. However, the existence of mixed systems does make it important to test all taps and appliances when the mains supply is turned off and not just a few representative ones. It's only a small precaution but it may save you from requiring a snorkel when repairing a pipe.

THE HOT-WATER SYSTEM

The cold-water storage tank in the loft feeds the hot-water storage cylinder. Every time hot water is drawn off at the tap, cold water from the cistern automatically flows into the cylinder to replace it.

The water may well be heated in the cylinder by an electric immersion heater. But usually the main source of heat is a boiler using gas, oil or solid fuel. As the temperature of the water is raised in the boiler it rises up the **flow** pipe and into the cylinder. As hot water comes in, the cylinder releases cold water through its **return** pipe and this goes to the boiler. Thus there is a circular motion of water being heated and replaced until a thermostat declares it to be of a satisfactory temperature and shuts off the boiler. A draw-off pipe to the hot taps is taken from the top of the cylinder where the water is hottest. In case the water is drastically overheated it can escape — with frightening noises — up the **vent** pipe which leads from the cylinder back to the cold storage tank.

As well as direct and indirect cold-water systems, there are direct and indirect hot-water cylinders:

Direct cylinder: This is simply a large collecting tank for hot water. Its weakness is that scale or fur builds up inside pipes in areas where the water contains lime and is described as being 'hard', and high temperatures make this problem worse. If the inside of your kettle is coated with a creamy white deposit then you have a scale problem. The result in the hot-water system is bubbling and banging, as water is forced through pipes that are growing ever narrower internally, and damage to the boiler. Using a water-softener and reducing the temperature to which the water is heated will improve matters but a better answer is an indirect hot-water system.

DIRECT HOT-WATER SYSTEM

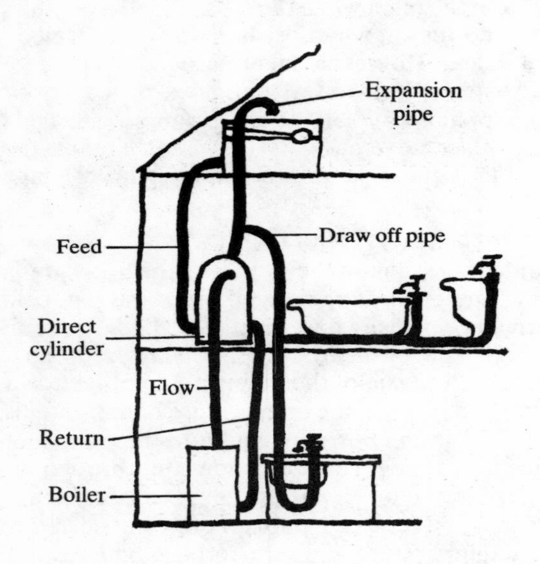

Indirect cylinder: This uses two circulations of water. The **primary** one is from the boiler to a large metal coil set inside the main hot-water cylinder, which the technically minded call a **calorifier**. The water in the calorifier heats the water outside in the main cylinder. This is then distributed to the taps in the **secondary** circulation. The primary circulation remains free from scale because the same water is used over and over again so there is no fresh supply of mineral deposits. Meanwhile, little scale accumulates in the secondary system because the water is cooler. Because the two circulations are separate each needs its own cold-water cistern, feed pipe and vent pipe.

INDIRECT HOT-WATER SYSTEM

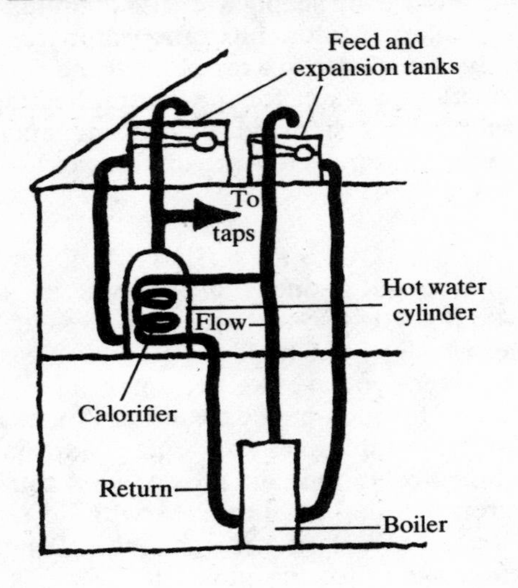

Self-priming cylinders work in a similar way to indirect cylinders but the two circulations of water in the cylinder are kept apart by means of an air lock. These cylinders will not need a separate feed and expansion tank. There are also self-priming packaged systems in which the hot-water cylinder comes with its own cold-water storage tank attached. These are particularly useful where there is no loft space, for example in flats. Conversion kits are available for turning ordinary direct cylinders into indirect ones by installing a calorifier.

The storage of large quantities of hot and cold water about the house has long been regarded as an example of typical British eccentricity by our fellow Europeans. While they have had mains-fed hot- and cold-water supplies that make cylinders and storage tanks unnecessary we have been hanging on to our beloved ballcocks and cisterns. In the past, one of the main obstacles in Britain has been the water authorities, who liked the idea of everyone having their own personal reservoir so that there would be no sudden shortages in periods of great demand. They were also concerned about contaminated water getting back into the main supply.

Now, though, the authorities have withdrawn their objections to direct supplies and we are seeing wide use of multipoint heaters and combi heater-boilers. **Multipoints** take water from the mains and heat it instantly in response to a tap being turned on. **Combis** do the same and provide hot water for the central heating as well. However, the traditional system does have advantages, particularly where the mains pressure is low or variable, and will be with us for a long time yet.

TOOLS OF THE TRADE

If you are going to set about your plumbing in earnest there are some tools you'll need — some basic, some less so. We'll start with the basic ones which will be handy in emergencies, the first type of plumbing experience you are likely to enter into.

Nuts are turned by open-ended **spanners**. An assortment of different spanners can be replaced by a couple of adjustable ones. While nuts are tightened or undone the pipe or joint can be held with an adjustable wrench called a **Stilson**. As with adjustable spanners, having both a small and a large set is desirable. In addition, a special **basin wrench** is handy for the nuts under sinks and baths where there is a shortage of space. Joints can be made watertight by having a sealing tape called **PTFE tape** wrapped around the threads. A screwdriver, pliers and a hacksaw will also be useful.

BURST PIPES

Water expands as it freezes and this tiresome trait is often responsible for making people confront their plumbing for the first time. The force of the frozen water can split pipes but this doesn't become obvious until the ice melts. Stopping the deluge is the first priority, and the first stopcock upstream of the burst should be shut. Copper pipes rarely split, but if they do a new section can easily be inserted. What normally happens with copper is that the joints are forced apart by the pressure of the ice and these will need to be remade (see the section on pipework).

Splits in lead pipes can be repaired temporarily by covering them with epoxy resin and binding with nylon tape, using a couple of layers of necessary. Very small splits can be made watertight by running hard soap into the crack and binding. Special bandages and clamping devices can also be bought to make this type of repair.

If the sudden absence of a water supply reveals that a pipe has frozen, you can thaw it out before any damage has occurred by using a hair-drier or by hanging a hot-water bottle on it. If a pipe is very exposed to frost it must be lagged, and it may be worth inserting a stopcock in front of it so that if there is any further problem it can quickly be isolated.

TACKLING THAT TAP

To install a new washer the first action required is to cut off the water supply to that infuriating dripping tap. If it is the kitchen cold tap the main stopcock is the place to do this. The same goes for other cold taps if the house is on a direct system. If not then you will need to isolate all hot taps and bathroom cold ones by draining the cold-water cistern. You can do this by turning off the main stopcock and turning on all the taps, but a lot of water is saved if you put a piece of wood across the cistern and tie the ballcock arm up to it so that the valve is kept shut.

PILLAR TAP

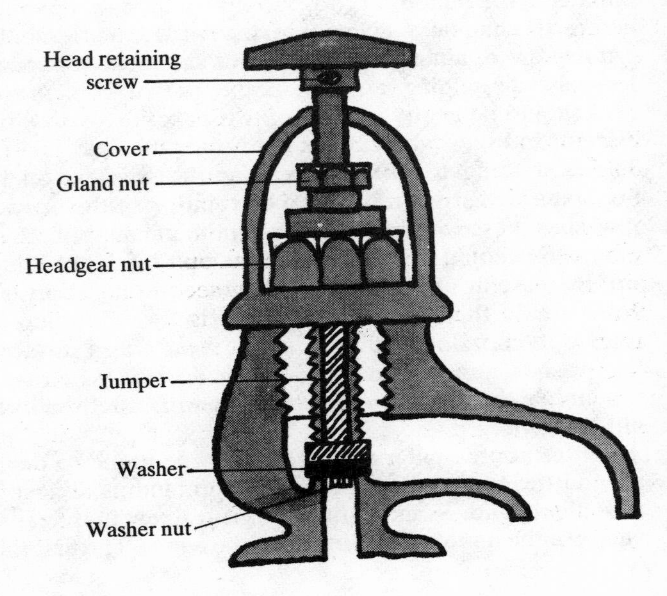

Even if it is a hot tap that needs a new washer the cold cistern should be drained. Then, when the flow has ceased, turn on the hot one, from which only a small amount of water will emerge. This avoids draining the expensively heated hot water from the cylinder. What has happened is that hot water is unable to leave the cylinder because there is no cold water pushing from behind.

Most bath and mixer taps need ¾-in washers, while the size for sink and basin taps is ½ in. Metric-size taps will need 15-mm or 20-mm washers. Take the appropriate washer and open the tap fully before unscrewing the cover if it has one. You may well be able to do this by hand, but if you have to use a wrench put a cloth round the tap first to protect the chrome. Under the cover you will find two nuts. The smaller top one is the **gland nut** and the lower, bigger one is the **headgear**. Unscrew the headgear and remove the **jumper**, the piece that carries the washer. The washer is attached to the jumper by a small nut. Remove it with a spanner while holding the shaft of the jumper in a vice or in the jaws of a pair of pliers. Replace the old washer with a new one and reassemble the tap.

Many taps of modern design have **shrouded** tops of chrome or plastic which at first appear to have been designed to defy entry. Some may be pulled off, others require the tap to be opened fully before the handle is given an extra twist. One design has a small grub screw retaining the cover. But the most common shrouded taps have a retaining screw under the 'hot' or 'cold' disc on the top. This should be gently levered off with a knife. With **mixer** taps it's difficult to know whether it's the hot or the cold that is dripping. The best thing to do is to replace the washers on both sides. **Supataps** are turned on and off by rotation of the nozzle. You can rewasher these without cutting off the water supply. The nut above the nozzle should be undone and the tap turned on. The water flow will increase at first but then be reduced to a trickle as the check valve inside the tap comes into operation. Continue turning to release the nozzle and tap the end of it on a hard surface to release the washer, jumper and anti-splash device. When reassembling remember that the nozzle screws on with a left-hand thread i.e. anticlockwise.

On traditional **pillar** taps water may be found to be leaking out around the top of the spindle. The problem is almost certainly a defective gland. Remove the tiny grub screw that fixes the handle and take the handle off. Now open the cover. The first thing to do is to attempt to tighten the gland nut but if this has been fully tightened the gland needs to be replaced. Undo the gland nut and use a knife point or other sharp tool to pick out the stuffing. Then repack the gland using wool or string smeared with Vaseline, winding it a number of times round the spindle. Alternatively, use PTFE tape. Many modern taps use rubber rings called **O-ring seals** instead of gland packing. They will be found under a removable clip on top of the headgear.

CISTERNS

Hot-water cylinders and WCs both keep a supply of cold water in a cistern, and a valve is used to keep the cistern full while preventing it from overflowing. The traditional method of achieving this uses the celebrated **ball valve**. This consists of a floating ball which used to be made of copper and is now made from polythene. When water is drawn from the tank, the water level falls and so does the ball. This action automatically opens the valve at the end of the arm holding the ball and water flows in from the main. As the ball rises to the top of the tank it closes the valve and the inflow of water stops.

Just as irritating as a dripping tap is a dripping cistern overflow pipe. These pipes provide an escape route for water in case the water supply is not cut off when the cistern is full. As a result the householder is alerted to the problem by water running down the outside wall and not by the unceremonious collapse of a sodden ceiling. Every house has as many overflow pipes as it has cisterns, and conventionally there will be one poking out around the eaves, which is from the cold-water storage cistern in the loft, and another further down the wall, which is connected to the cistern of the WC. If either of these is constantly dripping you have a ball-valve problem. It may be found that the only problem is that the ball valve has been set too high, allowing water just to reach the overflow. The answer is to remove the ball by unscrewing it and gently bend the arm down a little.

Scale and corrosion on the moving parts of the very common **Portsmouth** valve can often cause it to stick. To clean it, first remove the split pin that holds the float arm, using pliers. If there is a screw-on cap at the end of the valve, remove it. Inside the valve is a piston holding the washer. This piston must be taken out by means of a screwdriver or nail inserted in the slot under the valve body. Clean the plug with wire wool and smear it with Vaseline before reassembling. If the washer is worn it must be replaced. It is held in place with a screw-on cap which should be undone with pliers while the body of the piston is held firm by a screwdriver pushed through its slot. If the cap just won't budge it is possible to pick out the old washer and force a new one in place using a small screwdriver or knife.

If the ball itself has been punctured it must be unscrewed and replaced. However, you can make an efficient temporary repair by enlarging the hole in the ball so that the water drains out easily and then tying a plastic bag round it to keep it watertight.

Portsmouth valves are marked HP for high pressure or LP for low pressure. The high-pressure ones should be used on mains-fed storage cisterns and the low-pressure ones on cisterns fed from the storage tank. If an LP valve is used on the main storage cistern it won't shut the water off properly.

Croydon pattern ball valves are incredibly noisy and thankfully rare nowadays. If you come across one you will find it very similar to the Portsmouth valve except that the washered plug moves up and down instead of horizontally.

Many modern cisterns are fitted with **Garston** diaphragm valves. Instead of a washered piston the float arm pushes a rubber diaphragm against a nylon nozzle to stop water coming in. The most common problem with it is debris causing an obstruction which reduces the water flow. Unscrew the large cap nut by hand, pull out the diaphragm and clean it. You can adjust the Garston float by turning the nut at the end of the arm. A **Torbeck** valve has features of both designs and the float is the most simple to adjust. Simply move it up or down the end of the float arm.

Zinc galvanized steel cisterns connected to copper pipes will inevitably corrode as a result of electrolytic action, which works in the following way: where water is slightly acid the connection will create a very weak and rudimentary electric cell, and as the current passes through the water the zinc will slowly dissolve away. Creating one's own electric current may seem a wonderful stroke of luck to those who have to retire to a darkened room on receiving the quarterly power bill. But unfortunately this type of electrical activity will only cost you more money, for once the zinc is eaten away the steel underneath will rust. The answer is to paint the cistern with a bitumen preparation or protect it with the impressively named **sacrificial anode**. Different metals have different electric potentials and it is always the metal that has the higher potential that is eaten away. The anode is usually a lump of magnesium, as this has a much higher potential than copper or zinc. It can be placed in the cistern and 'sacrificed' while the rest of the system remains untouched.

Although a damaged steel cistern can always be replaced with a lighter and corrosion-free one made of fibre-glass, polythene or glass-reinforced plastic, it may be more economical to repair that rotting beast in the loft. Turn off the main stopcock and drain the cistern by opening the bathroom cold-water taps. A wire brush and even an abrasive disc may be needed to remove scale and rust which over the years can create monstrous growths that will leave a sensitive person feeling quite faint. However, work away and don't despair even when small holes appear in the side of the cistern. These can be filled with the epoxy resin that car-parts shops sell. Finish off with two coats of tasteless, odourless bitumen paint.

FLUSH FAULTS

The old-fashioned bell-type WC cisterns that are flushed with a chain are more or less fault-free apart from a deafening assortment of clanks and gurgles that can startle the deepest sleeper. Modern piston cisterns have an action that is much quieter and smoother but the washer (also called a flap valve or diaphragm) may sometimes need replacing. The symptom of an ailing washer is that the cistern no longer flushes at a touch of the handle. Members of the family learn to cope with the deterioration as it develops and acquire the knack of making a reluctant cistern flush. When an embarrassed guest emerges red-faced after a solid 20 minutes furious but unsuccessful flushing he is invariably told: 'Two quick, one slow and then surprise it with one more.' This is not a satisfactory state of affairs and the washer must be renewed.

WC CISTERN

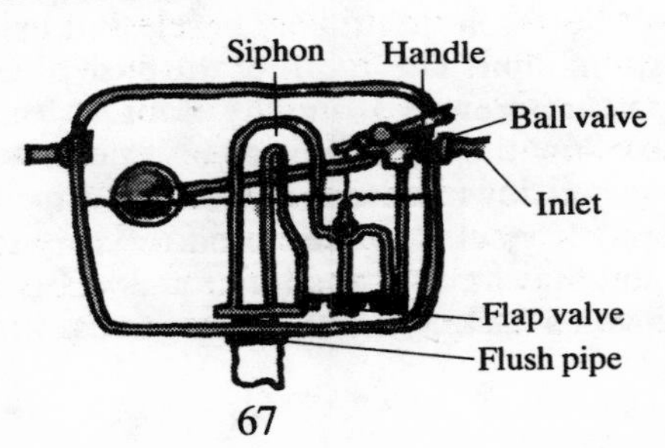

Tie up the arm of the ball valve to stop the cistern filling, and empty it by first flushing and then mopping up what water is left with a cloth. Undo the two nuts under the cistern and release the cistern and the flush pipe. Remove the flush lever linkage and lift out the siphon unit. Turn it upside-down and remove the disc that carries the washer. If a replacement washer of exactly the right size can't be bought then buy an oversized one and cut it to size with scissors. Trim it until it touches the sides of the siphon dome but does not stick. Some siphons are fixed with bolts inside the cistern. Others are not secured by a nut to the flush pipe but are pushed through a watertight O-ring seal.

Possibly even worse than a WC that won't flush is one where the pan refuses to clear. Check that there are no blockages (see the section below). If water is leaving the pan but solid waste is not there may be an insufficient force of water from the cistern. Most suites are the wash-down kind which need the weight and momentum of a two-gallon flush to clear the pan. Check that the cistern is filling to the correct level, i.e. to within an inch or less of the overflow pipe. The sides of the flushing rim of the pan can become obstructed with washed down flakes of rust or scale, and these can be cleared with the fingers. Using a spirit level, check that the pan is dead level. If it is not, pack the base with small pieces of wood until it is. Finally, make sure that the pan outlet fits squarely into the drain socket and is not obstructed by excess jointing compound used to cement it in place.

Few things in life are less pleasant than a leak where the WC pan joins the soil pipe. This is most common where putty has been used to make the joint and has become so hard and brittle that it cracks. The easiest answer is to dig out the putty, wrap a waterproof tape round the pan outlet and force it into the space in the soil pipe socket using a screwdriver. Fill up behind the tape with non-setting mastic filler and complete the job by wrapping more waterproof tape round the whole joint. The best solution, though, is to use a plastic push-on joint. This requires the flush pipe to be disconnected and the pan unscrewed from the floor so that it can be pulled forward to allow the connector to be fitted. Because the pan will often be washed down it should have been attached to the floor with brass screws. If steel has been used to save a few pennies you'll probably find they have rusted into the floorboards and will have to be cut free with a hacksaw. Don't forget to use brass to replace them.

AIR LOCKS

These can cause poor flow from hot-water taps or can even cause the flow to stop altogether after a short time, to the accompanying sound of hisses and gurgles. They should clear themselves because all the distribution pipes must be connected to the vent pipe and slope downwards from it so that air bubbles will rise out of the system. It is not unknown, however, for such pipes not to slope or to slope the wrong way.

The usual cure for an air lock is to connect a piece of hose with worm-drive **Jubilee clips** (which you can buy from a car accessory shop) to the kitchen cold tap, or to the one in the bathroom if it is directly supplied from the main, and the hot tap. Open both taps and the mains pressure will clear the air bubble. Air locks can also be caused by a storage cistern that is too small or a ball valve that is reluctant to open fully. Check this by getting someone to draw a bath of water while you observe the cistern. If it empties completely before the bath is full then this is where the problem lies.

The repetitive knocking that comes with the condition known as **water hammer** can be mistaken for an air lock but, of course, there is no interruption to the supply of water. It is often caused by the ball float of the cistern bouncing on ripples on the water surface and the noise being amplified through the rising main. The simplest answer is to stabilize the ball by hanging a plastic cup over the arm with nylon string so that it dangles in the water. The weight of water in the carton dampens the action of a skittish ball valve. More sophisticated solutions are to install a larger ball or to fit a Garston ball valve. Also check that the rising main is well supported and is not flapping about as a result of the pressure of the water running through it.

BLOCKAGES

Waste water that refuses to go away can be shifted by a variety of methods. The most common is the use of a **plunger**, a hemisphere of rubber or plastic mounted on a handle, which is thrust up and down over the waste pipe a number of times. Flexible curtain wire is often very good for poking out blockages. A more efficient form of curtain wire is a **plumber's snake**, a flexible metal spring 2 m (6 ft 6 in) to 5 m (14 ft 3 in) long and rotated with a handle. Motorized snakes or high-pressure water jets can be hired — and so can expensive operators who use much the same equipment.

Various chemical cures for blockages are available but they are really effective only on build-ups of grease. Drains are traditionally cleared with a set of rods that screw together. The old ones are made from cane but today polypropylene is used. They come with an assortment of heads that can be fitted to the end of the first rod.

When sinks and baths refuse to empty the problem is likely to be in the **trap**. This is the bend in the waste pipe in which a permanent level of water is maintained to provide a seal against drain smells. A drip in freezing weather usually results in a solid block of ice here and it must be gently thawed out. A slight blockage of the ordinary kind can sometimes be cleared if you place the flat of your hand above the plughole and force the water down a number of times. Otherwise try the plunger after first blocking the overflow with a cloth. If this doesn't work the trap must be opened, preferably with a bucket under it. Old lead traps have an access eye at the bottom which you will need a spanner to unscrew. Modern plastic P-traps and bottle traps unscrew completely. If the blockage is further along the waste pipe curtain wire can be poked down to clear it.

A blocked WC can usually be cleared with a plunger or with curtain wire. If the toilet refuses to clear, check outside by lifting the lid of the inspection chamber. If it is clear the blockage lies somewhere in the soil stack and must be rodded through. Households with small children may well find the cause of the blockage to be a toy flushed down the WC and caught in the trap behind it. This can be retrieved by hand although it is not the most congenial pastime. We won't relate the exact words of one plumber of our experience in the wake of his manually excavating the last remains of Robert the stuffed rabbit from the innards of the loo.

The first sign of blocked underground **drains** may be that you'll find yourself up to your ankles in the overflow from a gully or an inspection pit. Gullies can be cleared by hand or with a trowel and flushed through with a hose. No one wants to know about inspection pits until there is trouble. As a result the lids become cemented on with a tenacious mixture of soil, grass and moss while the handles rust away to nothing. Free the lid by clearing the soil with a small trowel and then insert a spade down the side to lift it. Before replacing the lid put a line of heavy grease of the kind used in car servicing round the edge of the inspection chamber to make sure the joint is airtight and to ensure that the lid is easier to remove next time.

Blockages in drains are usually caused by toilet tissue creating a dam after being caught on some obstruction. It could be that a tree root has disturbed the pipes or that vibration from traffic has led to a fracture. Often the cause is rough cement work in an inspection chamber. To clear a blocked drain you will have to use rods. The first rule of **rodding** is always to twist the rods clockwise; if you do it the other way they may come unscrewed and create a drain blockage of their own. The second rule is always to rod **down** the drain, so start at the flooded end. Remove the inspection chamber lid, screw several rods together and insert them into the murky depths. You will have to feel your way into the half-channel in the bottom and this will guide the rods into the drain leading from the chamber. Screw on more rods as necessary and keep pushing until the blockage clears. Before drastic measures are taken such as climbing into the flooded chamber to guide the rods into the drain, forget about the second rule and probe from the empty end. If the blockage is just paper it will clear itself as soon as a small hole is made, so be prepared to jump clear. Finish by flushing the drain through. A bath of hot water is ideal for this — and also for you if you wish to re-enter civilized society.

In older houses the inspection chamber nearest the sewer has an intercepting trap, similar to a sink's trap, and this is a common spot for blockages. If a blockage occurs between the intercepting trap and the sewer, the rod will be unable to get through the tight turn of the trap. However, above the trap will be a **rodding eye**, a pipe closed off with a stopper that will allow the rod to enter. First, of course, the stopper must be knocked out with a rod or stick and this can be a tricky job if the chamber is full of water. Even trickier is getting the rod to enter the rodding arm while being unable to see it. The best solution is to first empty the chamber with a bucket. It is quite likely that the cause of the blockage is the stopper itself which has fallen out of its hole and obstructed the trap.

DRAINAGE

If you have been forced to make use of the previous section you may have learned more about drains than you ever wished to know. However, we now complete your education and provide a guide for those blissful innocents who have never troubled their heads with thoughts of where all that waste water goes.

One of the less attractive legacies bestowed upon us by the

Victorian age is the **two-pipe** drainage system. Our forefathers devised a form of sanitary apartheid to keep the waste from WCs separate from the waste of sinks, basins and baths. The architects and engineers of that time were motivated by a fear of 'drain air', a phenomenon regarded as only slightly less terrifying than Jack the Ripper, and believed to be responsible for all kinds of malaises and plagues. As a result older houses have a soil pipe connected to the WC which empties directly into the underground drain. Meanwhile, baths, sinks and rain-water pipes empty upstairs into hoppers fixed to the wall and downstairs into a ground-level gully. From here the waste water is piped into the same drain as the soil pipe. This ugly and complicated clutter of pipes which often disfigures graceful old houses is intended to avoid back siphonage which occurs in this way: the rush of water down the WC soil pipe creates a partial vacuum behind it and this may pull the water out of a sink's trap. The smell of drains and even sewer gas can now enter the room through that sink.

However, since the last war the **single-stack** system has come into general use with none of the dire consequences that were predicted by traditionalists in drain technology. All the waste appliances are connected to a single soil pipe which is usually inside the building and has an open end poking above the eaves of the house to ventilate it. Back siphonage is avoided by deeper, 75-mm (3-in) seals on the traps and by close attention to the design of the system. Waste pipes should be kept short and laid at a slight incline. This is particularly important in respect of the wash basin, and if the branch is longer than 1.7 m (5 ft 7 in), a 38-mm (1½-in) pipe should be used instead of the usual 32-mm (1¼-in) pipe, or an anti-siphon trap installed.

Sharp bends must be avoided, and to avoid waste from baths, basins or bidets being obstructed by WC waste, no connections should be made to the soil pipe within 200 mm (8 in) above or below where the WC pipe enters it. If this is a problem a patent collar must be used to allow connections to be safely made at the same level.

Where waste water still discharges into a gully, say from a downstairs sink or a gutter, the pipe must enter the grille rather than stop short of it as it did in the old 'open' gully system. This greatly helps to prevent blockages and consequent flood warnings.

TWO-STACK DRAINAGE SYSTEM

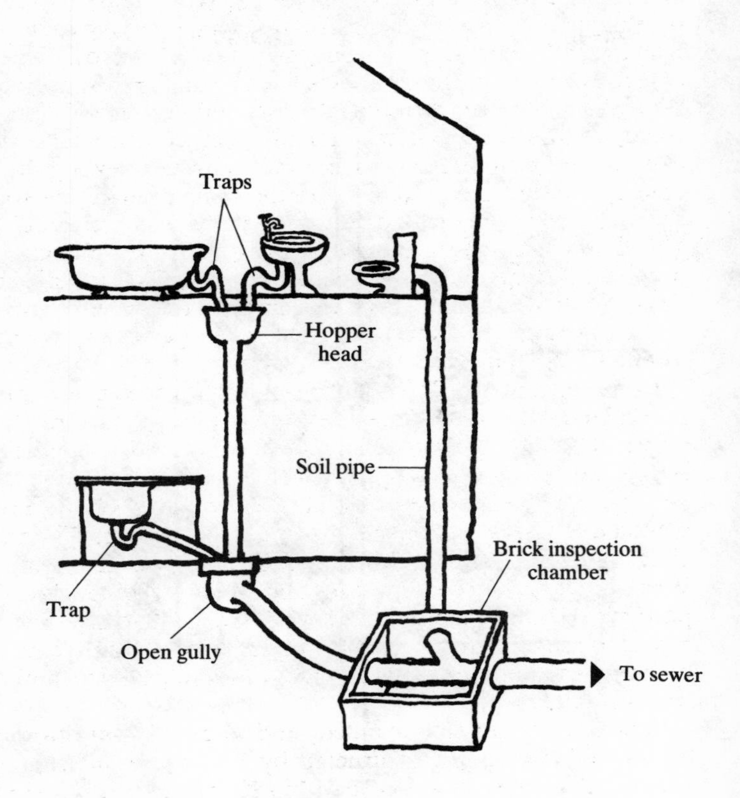

SINGLE-STACK DRAINAGE SYSTEM

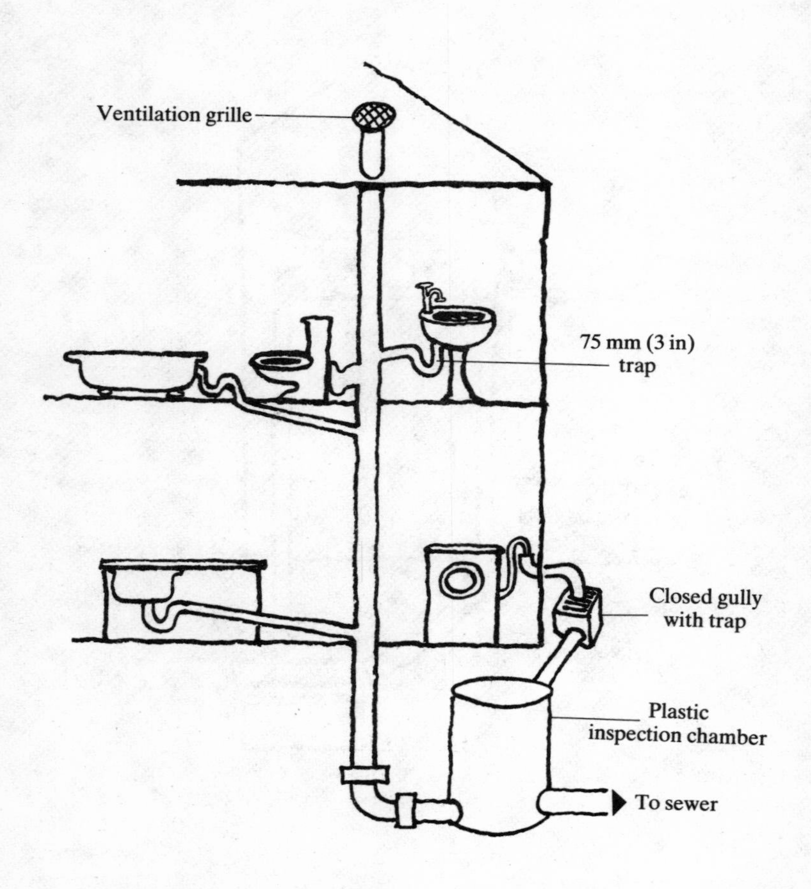

The pipe receiving the waste water must be large enough to take the flow. If that sounds obvious it has not appeared so to a number of professional and DIY plumbers. One bungalow owner recalls that soon after moving in he was flooded out with dirty soapy water. An investigation revealed that the shower, bath, kitchen sink, washing machine and dish-washer all emptied into a 1½-in pipe which then, even more perversely, went uphill to a gully.

Twenty years ago most houses were connected to the sewers by ceramic or cast-iron pipes. Nowadays ceramic piping is still widely used, with flexible plastic joints, but cast iron has given way to materials such as pitch fibre and uPVC. Most drains are constructed with 100-mm (4-in) pipes although if the slope from house to sewer is very gentle 150-mm (6-in) pipes may be used. uPVC pipe can be laid with less **fall** or incline than clay because its shiny inside surface carries the waste more efficiently. There is usually a collection and access point for the drains in the form of an inspection chamber (IC) near the house. If the inspection chamber is big enough to climb into it becomes a manhole. At one time ICs were brick built but modern ones may be made of pre-formed uPVC or concrete sections. It is common for old houses and some on modern estates to have a private sewer, although this may not be treated as an indication of status if announced at parties. Instead of each house being connected directly to the main sewer they all discharge waste into a single collecting pipe which takes it to the main sewer. The part of the private sewer crossing your property is your responsibility, and a blockage on your section will block everyone upstream and make you unpopular with the neighbours if you do not deal with it.

GUTTERS

Old gutters and downpipes were made from cast iron, wood or asbestos cement. Wood and cast iron ones are still made but the amount of painting they need has encouraged the relentless advance of PVC. It's light, easily fixed and the sections just push together. However, it is also vulnerable to knocks and susceptible to broken clips, and doesn't like having ladders rested against it. Plastic-coated steel or aluminium is stronger and both are available in standard lengths. Aluminium gutters can also be made seamless by being formed on site with special machinery.

The amount of debris in the average gutter is always a source of astonishment to anyone climbing a ladder. It invariably goes unnoticed until the gutter starts overflowing in a downpour, and should be cleared out once the rain stops. Sagging gutters are also likely to deposit water on your head as the water can't climb out of the dip. Check for straightness and for broken or missing clips. Holes in cast-iron gutters can be patched with car body filler and the gutter given a coat of bitumen paint. Leaky joints in cast-iron or asbestos gutters should be filled with mastic, preferably after you have taken the joint apart and cleaned it up.

CESSPITS AND SEPTIC TANKS

Whenever country folk used to gather the conversation would inevitably turn to warble flies and maypoles. Nowadays rustic pubs hum with the jargon of accountancy and chemical research. One subject, however, has been of constant and consuming interest over the years: the health of one's cesspool or septic tank.

Anyone buying a cottage out in the sticks, whether as a permanent home or for weekend use, may find that it is remote from any laid sewer and makes use of one of these medieval-sounding installations. The important thing is to be able to distinguish between them.

⋆ A **cesspit** does not solve a sewage problem but merely delays dealing with it. It is simply an underground chamber in which sewage is stored until the council or a private contractor comes and pumps it out for you. This service could be required every few weeks or every few months depending on the size of the pit and the size of the household. Since the sixties, the Building Regulations have specified a capacity of at least 4,000 gallons but traditional ones may be only a quarter of this size. They were designed to cope with just a kitchen sink and an outside WC, and are certainly too small for a modern house equipped with bath, bidet, shower, automatic washing machine and dish-washer.

⋆ A **septic tank** om cpmtrast, can be a very efficient means of handling sewage, if you'll forgive the expression. The tank is again an underground chamber but this time it keeps the sewage so that anaerobic bacteria — organisms that live without oxygen — break it down into an effluent. This is then filtered through a bed of coke, stones or clinker and during this process aerobic bacteria — those that do need oxygen — break it down further until it is harmless and can be discharged into a stream or river, or allowed to soak into the soil through a system of land drains.

Septic tanks can be brick built or made of glass-reinforced plastic. Always consult the council on deciding to install or replace one because different local conditions will require different drainage systems. Septic tanks should work for many years without needing attention but sludge should be removed every couple of years by the council or a contractor. One thing septic-tank owners must remember is to go lightly with disinfectant or there is a danger that all those diligent bacteria may be wiped out.

PIPEWORK

If your enthusiasm for plumbing mounts — or if disaster strikes — you may wish to advance as far as doing your own pipework, a task that is not as difficult as it may appear. The dark ages of plumbing, when only those tutored in the arcane arts could cut a thread on an iron pipe or 'wipe' a joint on a lead one, are over, thankfully, and now anyone can tackle pipework using copper, stainless steel or polythene and the simple joints used to connect them.

Once again, there is a tool-kit that goes with the willingness to embark on these exciting enterprises.

Pipes are cut with a hacksaw and it is essential to cut straight to ensure a good joint. A wheel tube-cutter does this for you. The **swarf**, or rough filings left after cutting, can be cleaned off with a round, half-round or flat file or with a special brush, and the end of a copper pipe should be cleaned with steel wool before being inserted into a joint. Emery paper is also good for smoothing rough edges. The ends of plastic pipes will need to be cleaned with a degreaser before they are glued with a solvent weld cement.

Slight bends in 15-mm copper tubing can be made over the knee. For tighter bends and with larger-diameter pipe it is necessary to use a mechanical aid to stop the wall of the pipe collapsing. Pipe-benders with the correct size-former for the pipe are the easiest to use.

Alternatively use an internal or external bending spring. Internal springs are often reluctant to emerge once inserted, and they should be well greased to aid retrieval. It also helps if you bend the joint slightly too far and then back a little before trying to remove the spring. Springs and benders can be hired for 'one-off' jobs.

Clips are needed to support pipework. Spacing on 15-mm pipe is usually 1.8 m (6 ft) on vertical runs and 1.2 m (4 ft) on horizontal runs.

Flux and a gas-canister blowlamp are necessary for making capillary joints (see below) and a flameproof shield is useful. Where it is difficult to turn water off it can be frozen in the pipe with a special spray and the ice plug will hold the water back until the job is completed as long as you don't dawdle. Other tools that are not specifically for plumbing will also be needed, and you'll find them invaluable for other jobs around the house. These include an electric drill, a saw for cutting floorboards, screwdrivers, pliers, a torch, a claw hammer, a club hammer, a cold chisel, a wood chisel and a mallet.

Common sizes of copper pipe are 15 mm for sinks, wash-basins and WC cisterns, 22 mm for baths and expansion pipes and 28 mm for the cold feed to cylinders. If the plumbing was installed before 1970 the pipes could be in imperial sizes such as ½ in, ¾ in, 1 in and so on. Metric measurements refer to the outside diameter while imperial ones refer to internal diameter. The 15-mm and 28-mm sizes will match with the ½-in and 1-in pipes but an adaptor is necessary between the 22-mm and ¾-in sizes.

There are three ways to connect copper pipe: with non-manipulative compression joints, with manipulative compression joints and with capillary joints:

★ **Non-manipulative compression joints** just require a spanner to make the connection. The pipe is cut and cleaned to a bright finish. Slip the cap nut onto the pipe and then the **olive** or brass ring that fits inside it. Add on the body of the joint and tighten up the nut, sealing the joint as the olive is crushed against the pipe by the pressure.

★ **Manipulative compression joints** are a little more complicated, but it is worth knowing about them in case they are discovered during the course of some repair. The joint body is slipped over the end of one pipe and the cap nut over the other. Then the end of each pipe is widened slightly by a special tool. A copper cone is inserted in the newly-created bell-ends which have been smeared with a jointing compound. The joint is then screwed up.

★ **Capillary joints**, sometimes known as Yorkshire fittings, are neater than the previous two and are easier to use in tight corners where there is no room to turn a spanner. The joint is made by solder, and pre-soldered fittings are the simplest to use. Cut the pipes squarely, remove all traces of burr and clean well using fine emery paper or wire wool. Smear flux thinly over the pipe ends and inside the ends of the fitting and thrust the pipes into the fitting as far as the pipe stop. Heat one side of the fitting with a blowtorch until a ring of bright solder is drawn by capillary action to the mouth of the joint. Then do the other side. If the fitting is close to paintwork or wood you'll need a pad of asbestos or fibreglass to protect it. And if two joints are close together wrap the one that is first completed in a wet cloth to prevent the solder from being remelted.

PIPE JOINTS

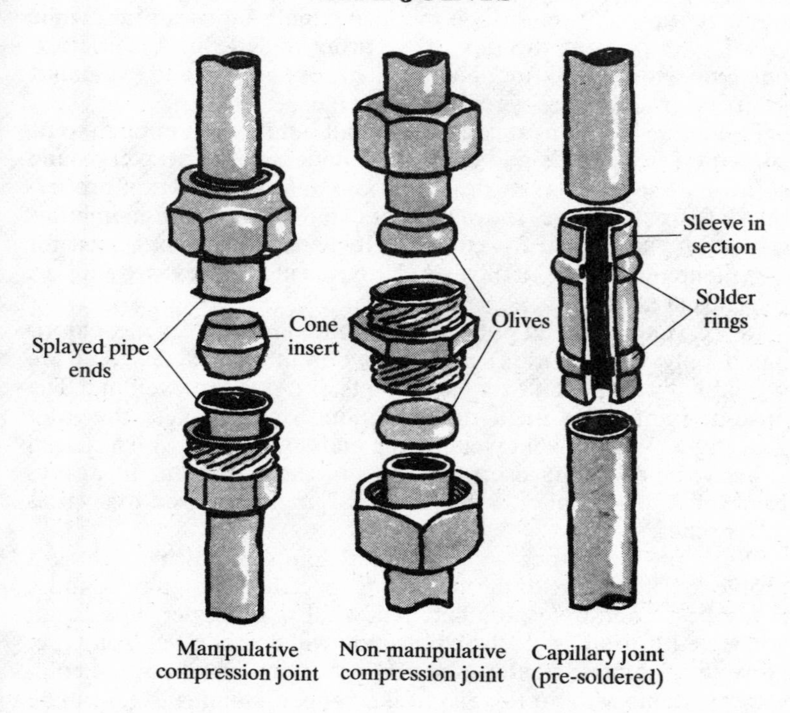

End-feed joints rely on your supplying the solder to the end of the fitting which is drawn by capillary action into the joint. If a presoldered joint hasn't quite worked it is possible to add some solder in this way. If this fails throw the joint away and start on a fresh one. Gadget fans might be tempted by a kind of electrically heated pliers which fit round the joint to warm the solder.

Various kinds of plastic pipe have been developed, particularly in America, to take both hot and cold water, but they are still making only slow inroads into the British market. However, plastic is simple to cut and joint and is invariably used for waste systems.

Polybutylene is suitable for both hot and cold supplies and can be joined with conventional compression fittings or with a special push-fit plastic fitting that resembles that used in a compression joint. A rubber O-ring inside the fitting makes it watertight while metal jaws prevent the pipe from bring pulled out again. Polybutylene withstands knocks better than copper pipe and expands if ice forms inside, thereby resisting damage.

Polythene has no heat resistance at all but it is soft enough to be cut with a sharp knife and is good for underground or overground cold-water supplies as its flexibility and natural insulation properties defy frost damage. It can be connected with compression joints similar to those used for copper. However, the fittings used for polythene require larger olives and internal metal sleeves to support the ends of the pipes.

uPVC (unplasticized polyvinyl chloride) and cPVC (post-chlorinated polyvinyl chloride) pipes can be cut with a saw and are assembled with push-fit ring-seal joints or by solvent welding. The push-fit joint relies on a rubber sealing ring to make the joint watertight. With solvent welding the ends are coated with a special adhesive before being inserted in the joint. Solvent welds are always used for water supplies, while ring-seal joints are used for waste-water pipes.

Work on iron pipes with threaded joints is much more of a problem. The cutting of threads needs specialized equipment and is really best done by a plumber. It is vital that copper pipe is not connected to iron as electrolytic action will corrode the iron pipe. However, stainless steel can be used to extend iron hot- and cold-water systems without this risk. Like copper, stainless steel can be joined with compression fittings although slightly more force is needed to tighten them because they are made of harder metal. Capillary fittings are also available for stainless steel but a special phosphoric acid flux must be used which can be difficult to obtain and can burn your fingers.

Lead piping is never used in modern homes but you may well inherit some. Given its age and the risks associated with lead, few will want to keep such a system. However, you may well be left with a few inches of lead rising main entering the house. It is possible for the novice to make the wiped joint that is needed to connect the lead pipe to a copper one but the best answer is probably to get a professional to make the connection and install a stopcock and take over from there.

INSTALLING APPLIANCES

This is where those impressive practical skills you've acquired are applied. This guide is necessarily brief and further research and close attention to manufacturers' instructions is recommended before starting work.

Showers: The traditional ones take hot water from the cylinder and cold from the storage cistern. The pressure will not be adequate unless the cold-water cistern is at least 90 cm (3 ft) above the shower head and to ensure this the tank sometimes has to be raised or even a new one installed. Where this is impossible a booster pump may be necessary. These showers will be usable only when water has been heated in the cylinder, and there are also problems of varying water temperature when water is drawn elsewhere in the house while the shower is running. A thermostatic mixing valve is the usual way of dealing with this. **Power showers** incorporate a pump to boost the pressure for masochists who like the sensation of being caught in a hot hailstorm. **Electric instant showers** are often easier to install and always provide hot water but the flow rate may not be as fast. They work by heating the water instantaneously as it passes through the device, and the hotter you want the water the less of it comes out. To keep the temperature and the flow up in winter don't go for a model of a less than 7-kw rating, and 8 kw is better. To install one, turn off the main stopcock, drain the rising main through the kitchen cold tap and cut into it at the nearest spot. Insert a **Tee-joint** compression fitting of the correct size. Make up the pipework with compression joints and don't forget to put a stopcock in at a suitable point to allow the shower to be cut off if necessary. The unit will require a cable connected directly to its own 30-amp fuse at the mains and a double-pole switch (see Chapter Six).

Washing machines: Some just run off cold water and have their own heater. In this case all you need to do is insert a Tee-joint into the main with a 15-mm compression fitting. Where the machine needs hot water as well a separate branch must be taken to the kitchen hot-water pipe, the system drained and a Tee-joint inserted. Some manufacturers specify that the pipework should connect directly to the machine. In many cases, though, the pipework should end in a tap or a special washing-machine stopcock attached to the wall about 30 cm (1 ft) from the appliance. Lengths of hose are then used to connect up. Where pipework already exists near the machine a self-cutting tap is an easier means of getting into it. A saddle is fixed over the pipe and as the tap is screwed in it cuts its way into the pipe as well. To allow the machine to drain the waste pipe can simply be hooked over the kitchen sink. A more permanent method is to provide a stand-pipe outlet of uPVC tubing connected to the soil pipe or to an outside gully. The stand pipe should be at least 35 mm (1⅜ in) in internal diameter so that the waste pipe is not a tight fit inside it, and it must be provided with a trap at its base.

Sinks and baths: Modern sinks and baths have combined waste and overflow units connected by a flexible tube which ends in a circular collar called a **banjo unit**. Fix the taps and waste fittings before installing the new sink.

Bed the waste unit (what ordinary people call the plughole) on mastic and then, working from under the basin, put on, in the correct order, the rubber washer, the collar of the overflow, the other washer or washers and the back nut. Tighten this while holding the plughole with pliers to stop it turning. Fitting the water-supply pipes to the taps can be a struggle in a confined space, so use flexible corrugated copper tubes which are easily bent into the ideal shape. These also get over problems with the taps being in a slightly different place. Make sure you get ones with swivel tap-connectors. These are simply screwed on to the tails of the taps while a compression joint connects the tube to the pipework. With luck the waste outlet of the new sink will connect the old trap. If not you'll have to buy a new one.

Baths are connected up in a similar way although the pipework is now 22 mm in diameter instead of 15 mm and the waste pipes measure 38 mm as opposed to 32 mm. Modern cast-iron baths have screw-type legs which allow the height to be varied. Pressed steel and plastic ones will have a cradle assembly.

Water-softeners: Hard water can be softened by adding sodium and calcium phosphates to the cold-water supply. But for a permanent answer a water-softener working by a process called **ion exchange** should be installed. This is hidden in a kitchen cabinet and connected to the rising main just after the pipe taking water to the kitchen sink, thus permitting the continued use of hard water for drinking. The water-softener may reduce the pressure to the cold-water storage tank, necessitating the replacement of the high-pressure ball valve at the tank with a low-pressure one. Check with the water authority that the type of installation complies with its rules.

6

ELECTRICS

'A smell of burning fills the startled air —
The Electrician is no longer there!'
(Hilaire Belloc [1870-1953]: Newdigate Poem)

A true story:

When troubled by a fuse that repeatedly blew and knocked out the power sockets, an elderly lady reached for the *Yellow Pages* and sought help from a criminal lunatic masquerading as a professional electrician. This man arrived at the house, wrapped 30-amp fuse wire a number of times round the offending fuse, charged £40 and left. The next morning there was a triumphant explosion from the washing-machine where the fault actually lay.

This chapter is aimed at stopping anyone being naïve enough to accept such a solution and then pay money for it. It may also encourage people to attempt electrical work themselves and this is no bad thing as long as the techniques are fully understood and the apprentice electrician is acutely aware of his or her limitations. Negotiate small jobs successfully a number of times before embarking on large ones and major work should always be checked by a qualified electrician. Because of the inherent dangers care and accuracy are essential.

TOOLS OF THE TRADE

Pliers can be used for cutting or trimming wires as well as for other duties, although a pair of side cutters or 'snips' are often handy. Both must have insulated handles. A large ordinary **screwdriver** and a small electrician's screwdriver with an insulated shaft are also necessary. A craft knife such as a **Stanley knife** is useful for paring off PVC sleeving from cables but on smaller wire this can be done with a pair of wire-strippers. A **torch** is vital and should ideally be one that has a square base so that it can be put on the floor to leave your hands free. A roll of **PVC insulating tape** is a must.

As in the case of plumbing, there is a range of tools that you will need to build up if you're serious about household DIY: an electric drill, saw and crowbar for lifting floorboards, a bolster chisel for cutting plaster and brick, a club hammer and claw hammer and a tape measure. It is useful to keep a supply of 3-amp and 13-amp fuses for plugs, and fuse wire or cartridges for the main fuseboard, as well as a strip of plastic terminal-connectors.

NEVER . . .

- Never work on an appliance that is plugged in. Once the cover is removed it is easy to touch the live wire.
- Never poke bare wires into a plug socket or try to jam them there

with matches. Even if it works, the earth will be poorly connected.

- Never forget to switch off at the mains before working on an electrical fitting, or to disconnect it by unplugging it. Simply switching the fitting off does not stop the live conductor reaching it.
- Never plug an appliance into a light socket. There is no earth and the light circuit could be overloaded.
- Never use an extension lead before uncoiling it. The coiled flex could overheat.
- Never run two or more high-powered appliances such as washing-machine and tumble drier from one socket with an adaptor. The socket will overload.
- Never have to waste time looking for the electricity board's emergency phone number. Keep it near the main fuse box or by the phone.
- Never forget where you've left the torch. Hang it up or keep it in a special drawer and make sure you've got spare batteries.

WHAT'S WATT

First, some definitions. Even if you never intend to apply this information it's worth remembering in order to take on DIY bores at parties. It may also prevent your being baffled when your money is at stake.

Electricity flows down wires rather as water runs down a pipe, and in the same way that water is pumped round a system electricity is pushed round a circuit. This pressure is measured in **volts** and in Britain this is standardized at 240 volts. The quantity of electricity being pushed down the wire is measured in amperes, commonly known as **amps**.

There is a natural resistance in the wire to electricity's being shoved down it and the amount of resistance is measured in **ohms**. The thicker the wire the less resistance there is and the greater the flow. Resistance makes itself felt by generating heat, and a wire that is too small for the load will overheat and even catch fire.

The amount of electrical power used by an appliance is measured in **watts** and will usually be marked on the appliance. To calculate the amp rating of a fuse, cable or plug to be used for a specific appliance, divide the number of watts by the number of volts. Thus a 100-watt light bulb needs 100 divided by 240 which equals 0.42 amps. The largest permitted flow of electricity through a three-pin plug is 13 amps. Appliances that need more than this, such as cookers and electric showers, must be permanently wired in.

People talk of an electrical 'circuit' because electricity has to make a round trip. It goes out from the meter on the **live wire**, enters the socket or appliance and then returns on the **neutral wire**. To use the plumbing analogy again, it is like water going round and round a central heating system. As a result there must always be at least two wires, the outgoing live one and the returning neutral one. A **short circuit** occurs when the live and neutral wires touch without going through an appliance.

Often there is a third wire, the **earth**. This is the vital safety feature of an electrical installation. If an appliance develops a fault, the outside casing may become live; if you then touch it, the electric shock runs to earth through you, with nasty results. But if the appliance is earthed, the power will run through the earth wire and blow the circuit fuse. Note that some appliances do not have an earth wire. This is because they are **double insulated** and there is no danger of the outside casing coming into contact with the internal wiring. Appliances with a low wattage, such as table lamps, may also do without an earth unless they are made of metal.

Electricity comes into the house through a thick armoured service cable carrying a live and a neutral wire. It is connected to a meter through a box containing the main service fuse. Neither the cable nor the fuse should ever be touched. The wiring beyond the meter is the householder's responsibility and it is here that the fuse box for all the household circuits is sited, together with a main switch for cutting off all the current.

There should be an earthing point at the meter to which all the other wires in the house are connected. The earth is usually connected to the metal sheathing of the electricity board's underground cable, or sometimes to a metal rod driven into the ground. Nowadays it is common to add a **residual current circuit breaker (RCCB)**, also known as an **earth leakage circuit breaker (ELCB)**. This will automatically switch off the current if there is an alteration in flow which indicates a fault.

There is a danger that if a fault occurs and metal piping becomes live the current may find its way to earth by a different route, i.e. you. To prevent this, all metal gas and water pipes, sinks and baths must be **bonded** to earth, which is another way of saying they should all be connected by earth cables to the main earth point.

FUSES

Fuses are deliberately designed to be the weak point of the circuit. When overloading occurs or a fault develops the current gets too high and the flex or cable becomes hot owing to its resistance. Because the fuse wire has a very low melting-point it breaks before damage can occur anywhere else in the system.

This melting-point can be set at different levels depending on what circuit or appliance the fuse is protecting, and so there are fuses rated at 5 amps, 15 amps and so on.

Cartridge fuses are the ones commonly used in plugs and are distinguished from one another by being of different sizes and marked with different colours. Fit a red 3-amp fuse for appliances rated under 700 watts and a brown 13-amp one for appliances rated higher than that. Cartridge fuses are sometimes found in the main fuse box but here there are traditionally **rewirable** fuses consisting of a piece of fuse wire connected to the two pins by brass screws.

If the fuse blows the wire will be seen to be broken and a new piece can be inserted and wound around the terminals and the screws retightened. Lighting circuits will need 5-amp wire, power circuits 30-amp wire, and a cooker may need 45-amp wire. Main fuse boxes are now being called consumer units and this is a more accurate term because many don't have fuses any more. Instead, they contain **miniature circuit breakers (MCBs)**. Each of these is a kind of switch that goes off automatically if the circuit is overloaded, and they are reset by the flick of a switch or the push of a button, but they won't work unless the fault is repaired or the overloading removed.

If a fuse box is being replaced or installed always opt for one with MCBs.

Fuses must always be of the correct rating for the job. Ingenious people with a taste for midnight fire-fighting have been known to replace fuses with a random assortment of items such as silver paper, baking foil and paper clips. The result is obvious. The 'fuse' will fail to break if a fault occurs and there will be an extremely dangerous overloading of the circuit.

CABLES AND FLEXES

Household wiring can be either a cable or a flex, and the different sizes are measured in square millimetres. Cables are oval and are used to distribute the supply about the house, through the walls, under the floors and up into the attic. If you remove the grey or white PVC covering you'll find three wires. One is covered in red PVC and is the live conductor. Another, the neutral, is black and the third is a bare copper wire which is the earth. These are typical sizes: lighting circuit 1.5 sq mm, ring main power circuits 2.5 sq mm, cooker circuit 6 sq mm, immersion heater 2.5 sq mm.

Flexes, not altogether surprisingly, are flexible. This is so that they can be easily used to run between plugs and appliances. Instead of having solid lengths of wire inside the insulation, they contain many thin strands twisted together. The colours of the insulation on the conductors are different to those in cables. The live is brown, the neutral blue and the earth has green and yellow stripes. This system of colour replaced the old red, black and green system and if any flex with these colours is discovered on an appliance it should be replaced at once on the grounds of age alone. Typical sizes of flexes for use on light fittings or small appliances are: up to 700 watts 0.5 sq mm, up to 1,400 watts 0.75 sq mm, up to 2,400 watts 1 sq mm, up to 3,000 watts 1.5 sq mm. Two-core flex has no earth conductor and is used only on double-insulated appliances and non-metal light fittings. Flexes used for kettles and irons are usually rubber insulated and textile braided to allow for the constant twisting they are going to get. Orange PVC-covered flex is used for extensions and outdoors, its bright colour making it easily visible and reducing the danger of its being cut accidentally.

Never join cables or flexes by twisting the ends together and wrapping a bit of insulation tape around them. Always use a proper junction box for power cables and plastic terminal blocks inside light fittings. And don't try to save a few pennies by using a junction box where a new length of cable is called for. Plug-in flex-connectors can occasionally be used when it is necessary to extend the flex, but in most cases it is better to use a single length of flex or to install a new socket near the appliance.

PLUGS

Modern plugs have three rectangular pins for the live, neutral and earth connections. Rubberized plugs should be used in places like workshops where there is a danger they may be dropped on hard floors, and waterproof plugs and sockets are available for outdoor use.

Manufacturers seem to spend a great deal of time making minute changes in design in their ceaseless search for the perfect plug, but despite the variations they all work in much the same way, and most people know how to wire one up.

For the record, here is the drill again: strip 5 cm (2 in) off the sheath of the flex using a sharp knife, taking care not to cut the insulation on the individual wires. Open the plug with a screwdriver, take out the cartridge fuse and loosen the screws of the three terminals. The green/yellow wire is the earth and goes to the terminal marked 'E' or '1'. The brown goes to the terminal marked 'L' for live and the blue goes to the 'N' or neutral terminal. Cut the wires to the right length and strip off enough insulation to allow the exposed wire to go through the terminal hole. Tighten the terminal screws and make sure the outer sheath of the cable is firmly held under the clamp where it enters the plug. Replace the fuse and screw the top back on.

POWER CIRCUITS

Houses used to be wired **radially** to provide power to sockets. Separate cables radiated out from the fuse box to feed a number of sockets, each on its own 15-amp fuse. The original radial wiring used round-pin sockets and plugs, but the absence of these does not necessarily mean that the system has been modernized. It may be that modern square-pin sockets have been installed on old wiring. Any radial power-circuit wiring that is discovered must be old enough to be unsafe and should be thoroughly checked by a professional.

Modern power circuits are wired on a **ring** circuit. Loops of 2.5-sq-mm twin-core and earth cable are taken out from the fuse box, round the house and back to the fuse box. This system provides more power as the electricity can flow round from both ends and it makes it easy for sockets to be put on the ring wherever is most convenient. Each circuit should cover an area not greater than 100 sq metres (1,076 sq ft) and normally each floor of the house will have its own circuit protected at the fuse box with a 30-amp fuse or MCB. This fuse will limit the power available to 7,200 watts. Radial circuits are still used to feed a direct supply to appliances that need

RADIAL POWER CIRCUIT

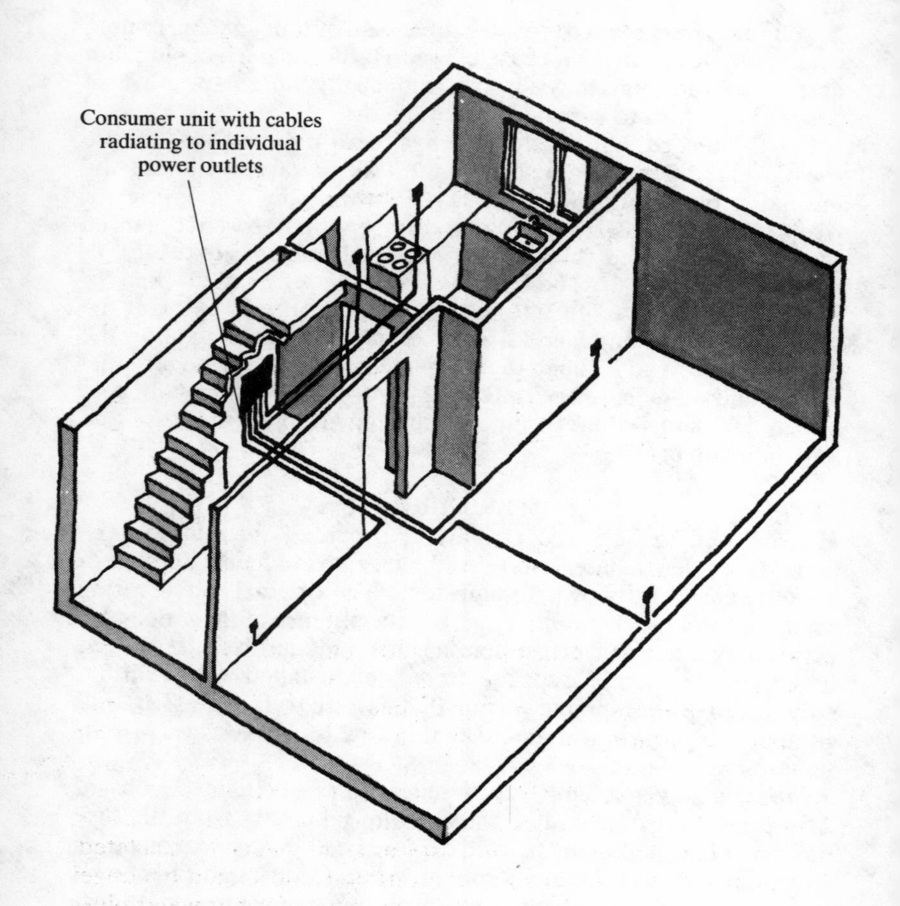

RING POWER CIRCUIT

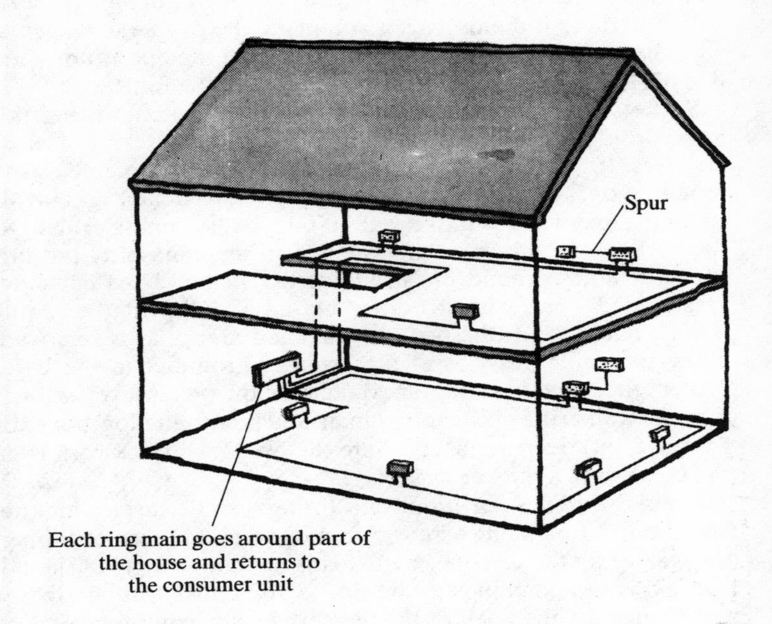

Each ring main goes around part of
the house and returns to
the consumer unit

a lot of power, such as cookers, electric showers and immersion heaters.

If you're proposing to install a ring main yourself, which is not an insuperable business, begin by drawing a plan of the floor to scale on graph paper and marking where the sockets will go. It's wiser to be generous with sockets than to have to add them later and it is just as easy to install double sockets as it is single ones. The cable should be drawn in on the plan and the amount needed calculated. Remember that to avoid voltage drops no cable should be longer than 80 m (260 ft), cables should not be run under hot-water pipes and they should not be grouped together.

It may be that when a house is being partially or completely rewired the fuse box is too small to take the required number of power, lighting, hot-water and cooker circuits. If this is the case a separate switch-fuse unit can be installed alongside the old one, or the fuse box can be replaced with a larger one. The electricity board will have to cut off the supply before this work can take place, and will undertake it themselves if you make the proper arrangements with them. If the box is being replaced, take the opportunity to get one big enough to provide spare capacity for the future.

Sockets were once often mounted on skirting boards but this is now considered unsafe as they are vulnerable to kicks and vacuum cleaners. Instead, put them on the wall where they can be **surface** mounted or **flush** mounted. Flush mounting is neater and involves sinking a metal box into the wall to take the incoming cable. Draw the outline of the box on the wall and, using a masonry bit, drill a series of holes around the inside of the shape. Then cut out the plaster and brick with a bolster chisel. Knock out the required 'knock-out' hole in the box, a weakened area that is removed to allow the cable entry, and fit a rubber grommet in the hole to protect the cable's insulation. Make sure the box is level and screw it to the wall using plastic plugs in drilled holes. Shallow boxes only 25 mm (1 in) deep are used where the plaster or brickwork is thin, but these have a thicker face-plate.

On plasterboard partition walls fittings can be surface mounted, and are fixed by being screwed to a convenient piece of timber in the wall or by the use of a cavity fixing anchor or toggle. The other method is to attach lugs to the side of the knock-out box that will hold it against the back of the plasterboard when the face-plate is screwed on. Use string or wire to hold the box in place until the face-plate is fixed.

It is simplest to take the circuit cable under the floorboards and through the roof space where possible. You can buy or hire a special device for cutting floorboards but it is not difficult to lift them yourself. First run a thin knife along the gap between them to check whether they are tongued and grooved. Tongues should be cut with a tenon saw. It is not unknown for professionals in a hurry to tear the boards up and break the tongues or smash them with a bolster but this is unnecessary and leaves unsightly damage. Find the end of a board, check that it's not screwed down, and prise a bolster or other suitable lever under it to lift it, shifting it gradually at a number of points before you prise it up. If the ends of the board are hidden under the skirting, insert a bolster at each side in the middle of the board and raise it enough to saw across it. Where the cable has to cross a joist, a hole should be drilled at least 50 mm

(2 in) from the top to take it. Notching the joist weakens it and leaves the cable vulnerable to nails. The cable should be fixed with a clip of the correct size.

Cable can also be surface mounted and just clipped to the wall or woodwork. Alternatively, it can be hidden inside plastic trunking or special skirting or coving. Even neater is to run it down hollow internal partition walls. However, sections of plasterboard will have to be removed to enable you to cut notches in the horizontal timbers or noggins. Feeding cable down the cavity of external walls is frowned upon, and obstructions such as wall ties, joist-ends and wayward chunks of cement make this an unrewarding occupation anyway. If plaster has to be cut to take the cable, use a sharp knife to score two lines 25 mm (1 in) apart, and then knock the plaster out with a bolster to a depth of about 20 mm (¾ in). The cable should always be run vertically or horizontally so everyone knows where to avoid banging that picture hook in. Many people plaster straight over the cable but it is better to protect it by covering it with plastic or aluminium channelling. Don't nail this into position because there is always a danger of hitting the edge of the cable. Instead use wide-headed nails such as plasterboard nails inserted at one side so that the channelling is just held with the heads.

A **spur** is formed when a length of cable is run off the ring circuit like a branch line. When an installation is being designed it will save cable if remote sockets are connected as spurs. Spurs are also an easy means of adding to the existing circuit.

The spur is taken either from an existing socket or from a junction box inserted in the ring cable. However, there are some crucial rules: never have more than one socket on the same spur, never fit more than one spur to the same socket and never fit a spur to a socket that is already a spur itself. Check that you are not on a spur by switching the power off at the mains and removing the plate from the front of the chosen socket. If there is only one cable connected to the terminals the socket is already a spur. If there are three cables, it is on a ring circuit and a spur has already been added. If there are two cables the socket is probably on a ring and this is the socket you have been looking for. But make sure by checking the sockets on either side because it is just possible that this socket is a spur on which another spur has — wrongly — been installed. Only if the sockets on either side also have two cables can you be certain you have found the ring.

A simpler way of checking is to use a circuit tester, which can be bought cheaply in an electrical accessory shop.

Where a spur is being added fix the new box first to make it easy to calculate the length of cable needed. Then switch off at the mains and dismantle the feed socket. Strip off about 50 mm (2 in) of the spur cable's outside insulation. This can be done with a craft knife but safer and simpler is the way the professionals do it: expose the end of the earth wire, grab it with pliers and pull back, splitting the insulation open. Now take 12 mm (½ in) of insulation off the red and black wires and cover the bare copper wire with green and yellow PVC sleeving. In the existing box there are already two sets of red (live), black (neutral) and earth wires. A third set is now added. Twist all the red wires together with pliers and connect them to the terminal marked 'L'. Do the same with the black wires and connect them to the terminal marked 'N'. The earths go in 'E'. Tighten the screws and check that all the wires are firmly held by gently pulling each in turn. Now go to the new box and repeat the operation. This time there is only one set of red, black and earth wires to deal with. Fix the face-plates to the boxes, switch on and test.

Where there is a shortage of sockets it may be easier to replace singles with doubles or 'two-gang' sockets rather than install new ones. No additional wires are needed as double boxes still have only a single set of terminals. The only complication is cutting a larger hole in the wall for the new knock-out box if the socket is to be flush mounted.

Fused connection units can be used instead of plugs and sockets to connect up fixed appliances ranging from cookers to clocks. They save constantly having to plug and unplug an appliance and make for a safer connection. The units carry their own fuses and often come with switches and red neon indicators to show when the appliance is on.

LIGHTING CIRCUITS

These are installed as radial circuits, usually one for upstairs and another for downstairs, each having its own 5-amp fuse back in the consumer unit. That means each circuit will carry a maximum load of 10 100-watt light bulbs burning simultaneously. That should be enough for anybody, but people keen on staging their own version of *son et lumière* are advised to install another circuit. For safety's sake no circuit should feed more than 12 lights, and a maximum of eight is preferable.

Lighting circuits can have **junction boxes** between the ceiling joists in which branches are taken from the incoming cable to the light and the switch. Recent installations use the **loop-in** method whereby all the ceiling roses of the lights are looped together by the lighting-circuit cable. Some lighting systems may use a mixture of loop-in and junction-box wiring.

LOOP-IN LIGHTING CIRCUIT

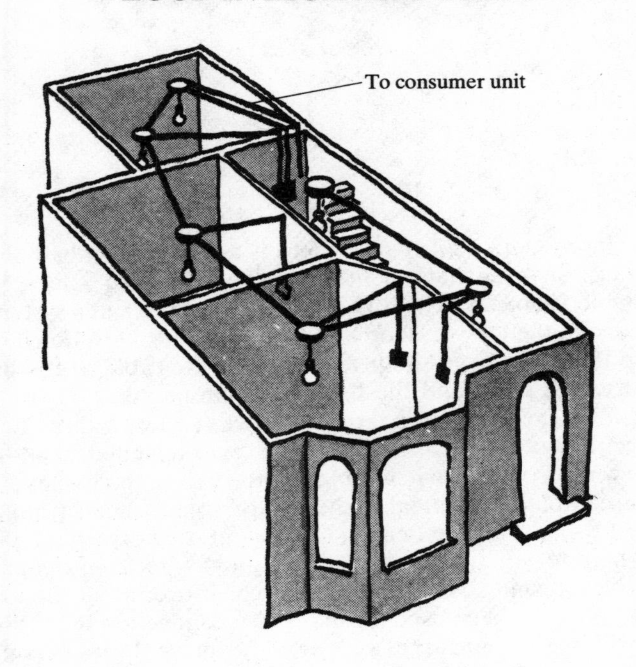

JUNCTION BOX LIGHTING CIRCUIT

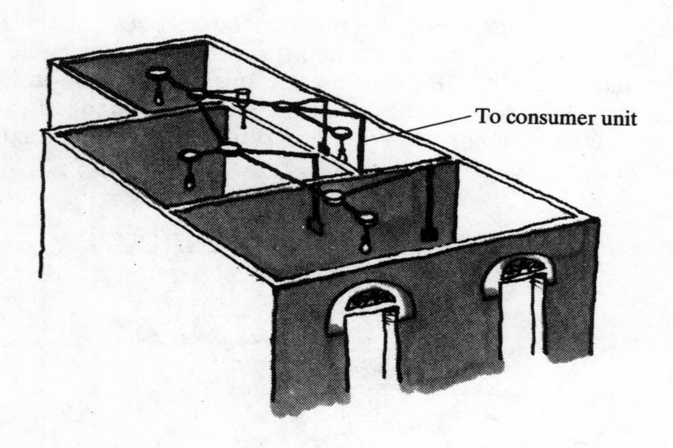

Inside the modern ceiling rose there is a **loop-in terminal block** and the mass of wires that meet there may lead you to believe you have stumbled across a British Telecom sub-station. But a systematic approach to the job will soon dispel any mystery. Arriving in the block are the cable from the previous rose, the cable to the next rose, the switch cable and the flex to the lampholder. There are three sets of terminals on the terminal block, two with three holes and one with two. The central three-hole set of terminals takes the live (red) wires from the switch cable and the two circuit cables. The second three-hole terminal takes the neutral (black) wires from the two circuit cables and the neutral (blue) wire from the lamp flex. The two-hole terminal takes the live (brown) wire from the lamp flex and the returning wire from the switch. If ordinary red, black and earth cable has been used for the switch connection the returning wire will be the neutral (black) one. This neutral wire becomes live when the switch is on and a piece of red tape should be attached to show this. But much better is to use specially designed **twin-red** wire for switches so there can be no confusion. There is a separate earth terminal to which the earths of the two circuit cables and the switch cable are connected.

LOOP-IN CEILING ROSE

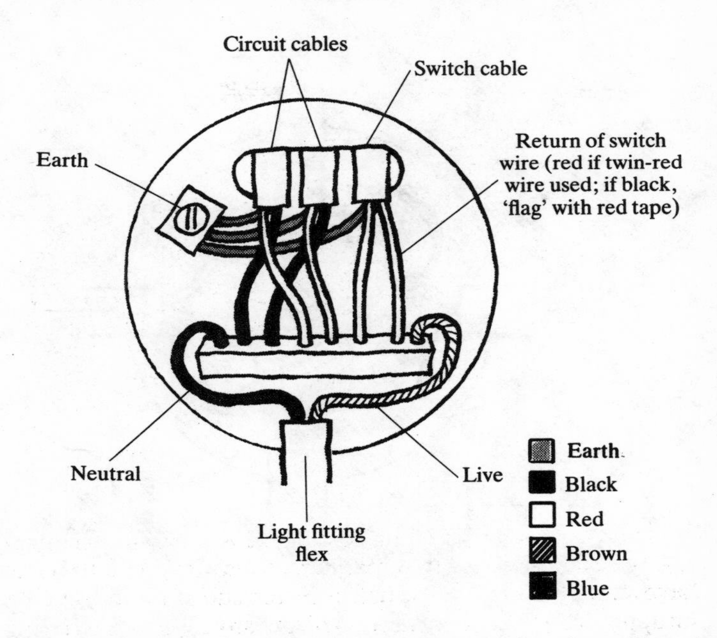

The base of the ceiling rose will have to be screwed to the ceiling. Make sure the screws have a joist to hold them or place a piece of wood between the joists. A hole can be drilled through the centre of this to take the cable.

The lampholder has just two wires going to it and it does not matter which way round they are connected. If the lampholder is metal, however, flex with an earth wire must be used.

In junction-box wiring the ceiling rose will be found to contain only one three-core cable and the two-core light flex. The cable will go to the junction box which will have four terminals. The incoming and outgoing cables will be connected to the live, neutral and earth terminals. The switch cable is connected to the live and earth terminals but the neutral goes to the switch terminal. Again this should be flagged with a red sleeve or tape if twin-red wire has not been used. The cable to the ceiling rose has the live wire connected to the switch terminal, and the other two to neutral and earth.

JUNCTION BOX LIGHTING WIRING

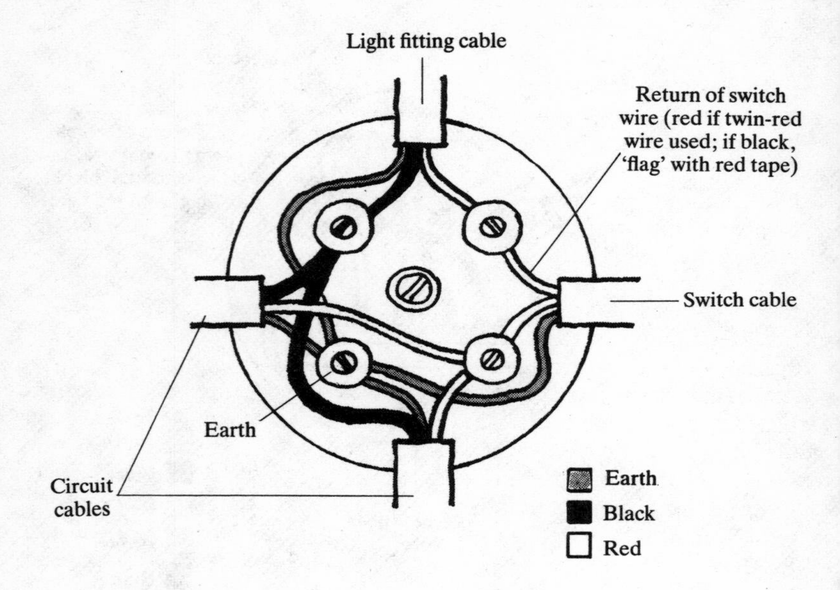

Some pendant and wall light fittings will need a circular conduit box to be recessed into the wall or ceiling. This is called a **BESA box** and is made of metal or plastic. The connections inside will be made using plastic terminal blocks which usually come in strips and can be cut off in sections of two or three. You can't just push the terminal blocks through the ceiling and leave them uncovered. The Wiring Regulations insist on the use of a BESA box.

SWITCHES

Switches are simply a means of interrupting the supply of electricity to the lamp or appliance. Instead of being taken directly to the lamp, the live wire of the circuit cable makes a diversion via the switch which is then used either to allow the electricity to flow through or to cut it off. Like sockets, switches can be surface mounted or flush mounted. One red wire goes to the terminal marked 'L1'. The second red wire in twin-red cable or the black wire goes to the terminal marked 'L2'. The black wire must be flagged with red tape to show that it is now acting as a live wire carrying the current to the light. The earth usually goes to a terminal in the mounting box.

Two-way switches are used for areas like landings where the light can be switched on and off from either upstairs or down. These have three connections at the back: 'C' or 'Common', 'L1' and 'L2'. To connect two-way switches special 1-sq-mm cable containing red, blue, yellow and earth wires is laid between them. The red wire goes to 'Common', the yellow to 'L1' and the blue to 'L2'. The earth goes to the earth terminals. One of the switches will also have to take the live supply. Bring this cable through a separate hole in the mounting box, connect the red and the black wires to the 'L1' and 'L2' terminals and the earth to the earth terminal. Screw the switches into the boxes, turn on the mains and test.

Dimmer switches can reduce or increase the brightness of the light to any desired level. They usually have a rotating wheel which also functions as the 'off' switch. Some have a separate on-off switch so that the dimmer can be left at a set level. **Pull-cord** switches are used where there is a danger a switch may be operated with wet hands, for example in the bathroom. The connections inside the switch are just the same but it is mounted on a pattress that is screwed to the ceiling.

Double-pole switches isolate both the live and the neutral connectors and are often used in fused connection units.

APPLIANCES

Cookers, immersion heaters and electric showers each have their own radial circuit.

Cookers rated at up to 11 kW need 6-sq-mm cable and a 30-amp fuse at the consumer unit. Those rated above 11 kw need 10-sq-mm cable and a 45-amp fuse. Free-standing cookers need a double-pole switch in the kitchen. From this switch the cable runs down the wall to a terminal outlet box and from there goes to the cooker terminal block where it should be firmly held under the clamp. Cookers are the only appliances permitted under the Wiring Regulations to be connected up with cable instead of flex. The oven and hob of a split-level cooker can be controlled from one switch unit but neither appliance should be more than 2 m (6 ft 6 in) from the switch. The cable can go first to one and then to the other, or two separate cables can be taken from the control unit.

Electric showers rated at 7 kW will also need 6-sq-mm cable, but those rated higher than that should have 10-sq-mm cable. Both will need a 30-amp fuse and a double-pole switch. If the switch is wall mounted it must be placed outside the room. Alternatively a cord-operated switch can be used inside the room. This can be surface mounted on the ceiling or flush mounted using a BESA box.

Immersion heaters come in different sizes to suit different cylinders. Some are designed to be inserted vertically from the top of the cylinder while others come as a pair to be installed horizontally at the top and bottom of the tank. The thermostat on immersion heaters is under the metal cover of the heater and it can be adjusted to the required setting with a small screwdriver. Immersion heaters need a 20-amp double-pole switch, 2.5-sq-mm heat-resistant cable and a 15-amp fuse at the consumer unit.

Electric doorbells either use batteries or need to be connected to the mains via a transformer. Using 1-mm twin-core and earth cable, take a spur from the ring main using a 3-amp fused connection unit and connect it to the transformer. Alternatively, use a spare 5-amp fuseway in the consumer unit. Take 2-amp twin-core bell wire from the transformer to the bellpush and from there to the bell. Some transformers have the three outlets marked 4 and 8 volts. Make sure you get the right voltage combination when you wire up your bell.

Shaver sockets are the only kind of socket allowed in the bathroom. This is because they have a transformer which means there is no mains supply in an area where operating an appliance with wet hands could be dangerous. They also have a device that restricts the supply to 20 watts and prevents any other appliance from being used on it. Shaver units without transformers are available for use in other rooms. They can be installed using a spur from the ring main using 2.5-sq-mm cable, or from a junction box or ceiling rose on the lighting circuit using 1-sq-mm cable.

A socket panel which will take a number of plugs simultaneously can be used where a number of small appliances are constantly plugged and unplugged into a single socket. The panel is simply plugged into an existing power socket and has its own circuit breaker to make it cut out if it is overloaded.

OUTDOORS

If you need a permanent supply to the garden or an outbuilding it should have its own main switch in the house and a residual current circuit breaker. **Never run a spur from the house**. Ordinary 2.5-mm PVC-sheathed cable can be used underground if it is protected inside galvanized steel or a plastic conduit. Alternatively use **MICC (mineral insulated copper-covered)** or **armoured-PVC-sheathed** cable, but both these need special fittings at each end to grip the metal sheathing and form the earth connection. All cables should be buried at least 500 mm (1 ft 8 in) under the ground. Ordinary PVC cable can be used for an overhead connection, but it must be at least 3.5 m (11 ft) above the ground and 5.2 m (17 ft) if it crosses the driveway. A span of more than 3.5 m (11 ft) must be supported on a **catenary** wire, and special wire and strainer bolts can be bought for this purpose. In the outside building the cable should end with a fused main switch, and socket outlets are wired from here. If you want an electric pump to drive a fountain in a pond, it should have a waterproof junction box to which the cable is connected, but a safer option is to install a transformer and run a 12-volt supply.

7

DEALING WITH WOOD

'In early times very little that resembles modern joinery was known; every part was rude and joined in the most artless manner.'
*(*A Manual of Practical Carpentry and Joinery, *1824)*

'The doors won't shut, or if they do there's a two-inch gap, the skirting boards have come away from the wall and the window frames have warped.'
(Owner of new house, 1987)

However much technology upstages tradition, complaints about poor joinery and poor timber go doggedly on. It is likely that the first hominoid to fasten two sticks together fielded criticisms with the time-honoured riposte: 'You can't get the wood these days.'

The problem with timber is that unlike many other building materials it continues to move, contract and expand in response to heat and humidity for years after it has been cut down, sawn up and dried.

The carpentry manual of 1824 cited above recommends that when skirting boards are to be installed they should be only lightly fixed. Then 12 months later the joiner should return to make adjustments for any movement that has taken place and fix them permanently.

Few tradesmen would consider this today. The historical answer to the problem was panel-and-frame construction. The panel is held in grooves in the frame which allow it to expand and contract without splitting as a solid piece of timber would do. The modern answer is to dismantle wood into veneers or chips and glue them back together in the form of a stable board. However, timber is still widely used in its raw state in house construction and fittings.

TOOLS OF THE TRADE

The traditional woodworker's toolbox contains a general purpose saw and tenon saw, a brace and a selection of bits for making holes, a medium-sized smoothing plane, several sizes of bevel-edged chisels, a mallet, a claw hammer, pincers, a try-square for drawing a line at right angles, an oilstone for sharpening planes and chisels, a couple of screwdrivers (a pump-action one saves a sore wrist when a lot of screws have to go in), a bradawl for starting holes and some G-cramps for holding work. Some kind of work-bench boasting a vice is vital, although a Workmate or even trestles will serve for very basic woodwork.

This is a bare minimum. The modern woodworker is able to replace or complement these with a range of power tools. Electric drills, jigsaws, circular saws, routers, planers and sanders all make life easy for the person who can afford them. And although 'professional' quality power tools can cost many times more than cheap DIY ones, they will outlast them to a proportionate degree, and survive hard work and rough treatment much better.

. . . AND USING THEM . . .

Measuring is the key to success at woodwork. 'Measure twice and cut once' is the old rule and it certainly saves creating a lot of expensive kindling. Marking cutting lines is traditionally done with a pencil but a biro or craft knife will give a much clearer and finer line to work to. Always mark the waste side of the wood and cut on that side of the line, but don't wander too far from it or there will be a lot of planing to do. A good cabinetmaker should be able to mark a line with a knife and cut leaving half a 'V' on the wood. Mark the start of the cut by drawing the saw backwards across the wood. Make yourself comfortable and then get to work, constantly checking that the cut is on line and vertical. A chisel can be hit with a mallet or the wood can be pared away. Always keep both hands behind the chisel — that is don't hold the chisel with one hand and the wood with the other or you are likely to find yourself hunting for bits of yourself in the sawdust.

Planes usually have a wheel with which to adjust the depth of the blade. Don't set this too deep in an attempt to remove wood quickly. It is just as quick and much easier on the arms to make a number of fine cuts with a keen-edged plane. Make sure the plane is held square and make long steady cuts rather than short frantic ones. Check for squareness with the try-square after each cut. Planes, saws and chisels must be kept razor sharp if they are to do the job properly. A professional may sharpen a chisel several times a day, but the amateur will do it once a year and then complain that the tool is no use. There is an art to sharpening tools on an oilstone or grindstone which only practice will provide. Patent devices which hold chisels and plane blades at the correct angle will make the job easier for the inexperienced and the teeth of saws can be 'set' or put at the right angle with special pliers and sharpened with a triangular file.

WHICH WOOD?

Household timber falls into three categories according to use: **structural**, such as roof timbers and joists, **non-structural**, such as doors, window frames, architrave, skirting boards and shelving, and **furniture**. All structural timber in houses must be 'stress graded', indicating that it is of high quality, and it should be impregnated with chemicals to give high resistance to rot, insect attack and fire.

Wood can be either **hard** or **soft**. This distinction is made on the basis of the cell structure of the timber and although hardwoods are generally hard and softwoods soft, this does not always apply. Balsa is classified as a hardwood and the extremely tough Parana pine is a softwood. Most of the timbers used in houses are softwoods, such as Douglas fir, hemlock, redwood and pine. Hardwoods like oak, ash, beech, mahogany, iroko and afrormosia can be used in construction but their usual role is in furniture or hardwood windows and doors.

Traditionally timber is sawn into planks and left to dry naturally. This is still believed by many to be superior to modern kiln drying in which a kind of oven is used to drive the surplus moisture out of the wood, but it isn't so. Not only is a kiln much faster, but the drying can be carefully controlled to produce superior results.

Softwood is sold **rough sawn**, **planed all round** or **planed both sides**. The sizes of planed timber are **nominal** as they refer to the dimensions it was sawn to. Planing both sides can remove 6 mm (¼ in) from the nominal size.

Hardwood is generally bought as it leaves the sawyard in large planks with a **waney edge**, wood to which the bark is still attached. Most yards will saw and plane the planks to order, but charges vary enormously for this service and should be agreed first. Hardwood and softwood is usually sawn **through and through**, sliced like a loaf down the length of the trunk. More expensive and more wasteful but much less prone to warping is **quarter-sawn** timber, planks cut radially from the centre. This method is used only with high-quality hardwoods.

Avoid buying timber over the telephone. Inspect it personally for defects, look along it to check for excessive twists or bends and spend time selecting the best of the bunch. Beware of:

Damp: Wood kept under an open-sided shelter may contain up to one-fifth of its weight of water. This level will fall to less than 10 per cent in timber kept indoors in heated premises. If excess damp is suspected, store the timber flat in a dry place for a week or longer before using it.

Knots: If they are loose or have a black surrounding ring they are called **dead** and the wood should be avoided. **Live** knots, which are usually smaller and show no sign of becoming separated from the timber, are acceptable.

Cup shakes: These occur in timber that has started splitting along the line of the grain causing sections to separate and curl across the plank. However, most timber will have **end shakes**, splitting at the ends due to faster drying out. These are normal and should just be cut off. The remaining timber will be perfectly sound.

Resin: Many softwoods, particularly whitewood and redwood, will have resin pockets. When these are small they can be sealed with **knotting**, but if large they should be avoided.

Mould: Softwood may also have blue stains from a mould growth. This is disfiguring but not weakening and should be treated with a preservative.

BOARDS

The tendency of sliced-up sections of tree to shrink and split has encouraged the development of board materials which do not do this, and which have the advantage of being available in large sheets.

Plywood is made from a number of veneers (very thin slices of timber) glued together. The sandwich can have up to 15 or more layers and always has an odd number. The reason for this is that the sheet in the centre has to be balanced by those on each side. If one layer moves, that action is opposed by the one on the other side. In fact plywood is still liable to warp because no two veneers are exactly the same. Also heating or wetting one side will produce contraction or expansion of the surface layer of veneer that will deform the board.

Ply is graded according to the quality of the outside veneer. ‘A’ means that both sides are perfect, ‘B’ that there are small knots or marks, while ‘BB’ indicates that dead knots and other faults have been cut out and patched.

Boards marked ‘INT’ are for interior use, ‘EXT’ are for outside and have been constructed with waterproof glue, while ‘WPB’ indicates that the boards are weatherproof and boil-proof. Marine ply is for boatbuilding and is made to very high specifications. Ply can be bought with a hardwood face for decorative effect.

Hardboard is made from softwood pulp that has been pressed into sheets which can range in thickness from 2mm (1/16 in) to 12 mm

(½ in). It comes in a variety of finishes such as perforated, enamelled, moulded, embossed and plastic-laminate faced. Where it is required to line damp walls, floor or ceilings, **tempered** hardboard which has been impregnated with oil should be used. If the board is to be used as an underlay for floor tiles or carpet it should be **conditioned** first to avoid buckling. Lay it down, scrub a litre of water into the back and leave it flat for 48 hours.

Blockboard is made from rectangular strips of softwood bonded together and surfaced by one or two layers of birch or mahogany veneer. Because the core runs the length of the board it is stronger that way than it is across the width. Single-veneer blockboard is likely to show the core in a series of ripples, but this is avoided by the use of a double veneer.

Laminboard is a blockboard with a much narrower core.

Chipboard is cheaper than blockboard or plywood and is made from resin-coated particles of wood that have been pressed together under heat. The **multi-layer grade** is of maximum strength, while the **painting grade** has very fine sanded particles on the faces. **Flooring-grade** chipboard has the edges machined so that the boards slot together and resist movement at the joins. **Faced** varieties are used for worktops and furniture. Chipboard is liable to bow if it is not well supported and needs special screws or inserts for fixing. Ordinary screws and nails will tend to come out as the board crumbles around them.

Medium-density fibreboard (MDF) is like a posh and more versatile chipboard. It has been widely used in the furniture industry and is now available for domestic use. It is made from fibres that are produced when timber is subjected to a vacuum and are then resin bonded and rolled out. Unlike chipboard it can be cut cleanly with a saw or machined, it takes nails, screws and glue like ordinary timber and the surface can be stained, polished or painted.

JOINING WOOD

The traditional method of linking two bits of wood together is to cut chunks off them to make an interlocking joint. The range of variations is vast, but the most common are the dovetail, mortise and tenon, lap and housing joints (see illustration). However, Chippendale-like skills are not required to do competent woodwork. A mortise and tenon may look neater but a glued and screwed joint can be just as strong. Drilling each piece of wood and joining them with glued dowels is neat, strong and simple to do if a dowelling jig is used to make sure the holes are accurately placed.

Glues: Modern glues create a bond that is stronger than the wood itself. For indoor work use the common white PVA-based glue that sets in about 20 minutes and takes about a day to cure completely. For work that must resist the weather use a urea formaldehyde such as Cascamite or Aerolite, formulations that were originally used in the days of wooden aircraft. Even more waterproof are the resorcinol formaldehydes that are used in boatbuilding and these can be bought from chandlers and yacht suppliers. However, they are expensive and can stain the wood.

Nails: Round-headed nails are used in most carpentry but oval heads are neater and can be punched in so that the heads are hidden. Cut nails are crude but grip well. Panel pins and 'lost head' nails have small heads that can be punched below the surface and are used in good joinery. Special tapered-head pins are used for hardboard. Screw nails have a twist running their length and hold better than conventional ones. Masonry nails are very hard and are designed to be driven into brick and block. A sprig is a headless tack for holding glass in window frames.

Screws: These come with either slotted or cross-cut heads, and are usually countersunk into the wood, which means you must first use a drill with a countersink bit to cut a dished 'seating' for the screw head to bed into. Double-thread screws can be inserted more quickly and save wear and tear on the wrist. Use brass, zinc, aluminium or stainless steel screws for outdoor work. Round or cheese-headed screws are used for attaching plastic or metal to wood.

Pins, blocks, bolts and plugs: Easy joints are also made with corrugated fasteners or 'wriggle pins', flat or angled metal brackets which are screwed to the timber, and with plastic blocks. The latter are commonly used to assemble chipboard kitchen units but they can be bought from DIY shops for other purposes. For heavy loads large timbers can be joined with coachbolts, which are bolts with a section of square shank so that the bolt can't turn in the wood while the nut is being tightened on the other end.

Any number of clever spring and gravity toggles have been devised to fix wood or other materials to hollow stud walls. Plastic plugs should be used to fix screws in bricks, while blocks require cellular plugs with fins to stop them turning. Plastic filler can be used to plug a ragged hole in a block wall before the screw is inserted. Wall anchors are bolts that are held fast by a sleeve which expands as the nut is tightened.

'UNOFFICIAL JOINTS'

Glue and screw

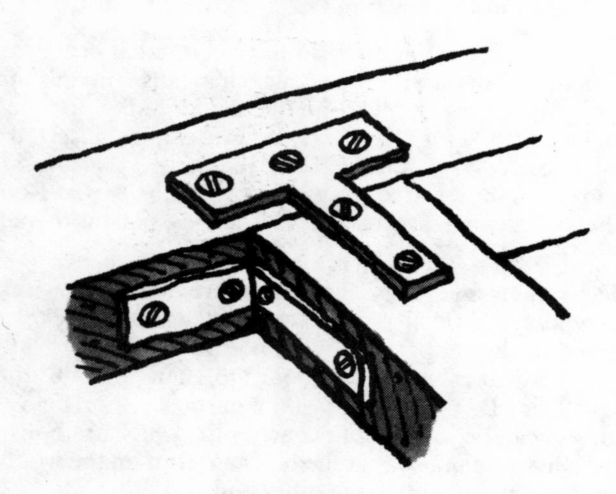

Metal brackets

Nailed and glued
plywood bracket

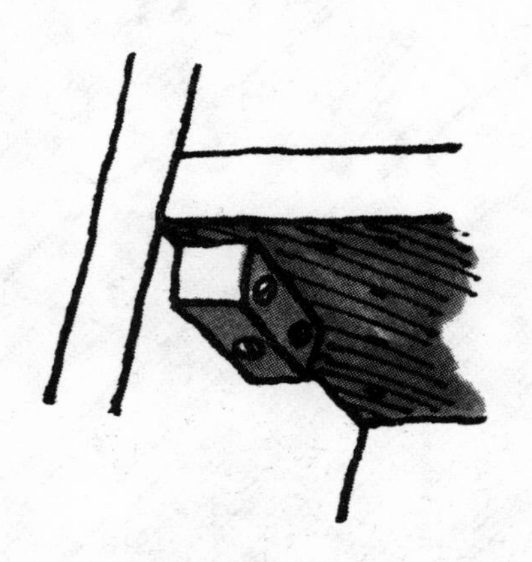

Plastic (or wood) block

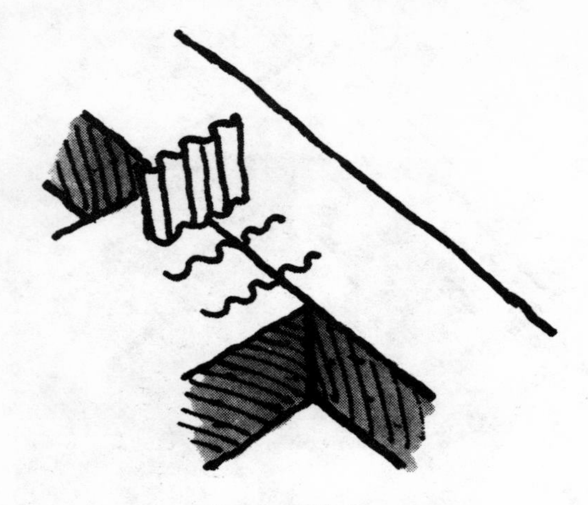

Corrugated fastener

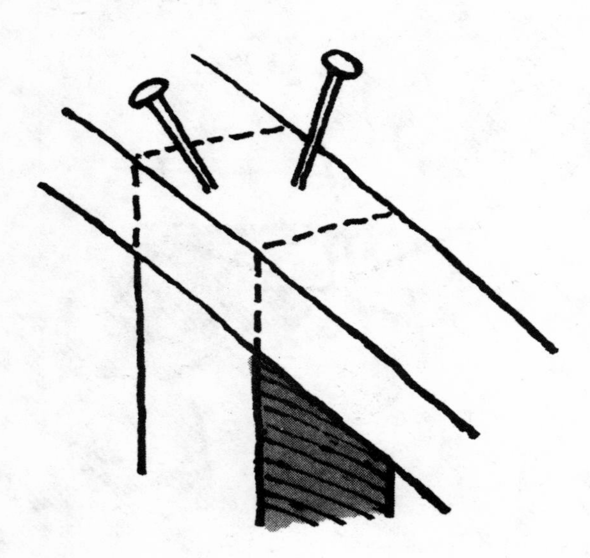

Skew nailed

'OFFICIAL JOINTS'

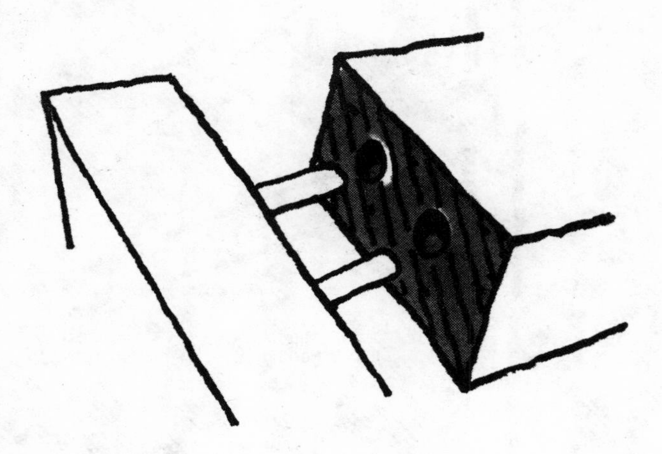

Dowelled

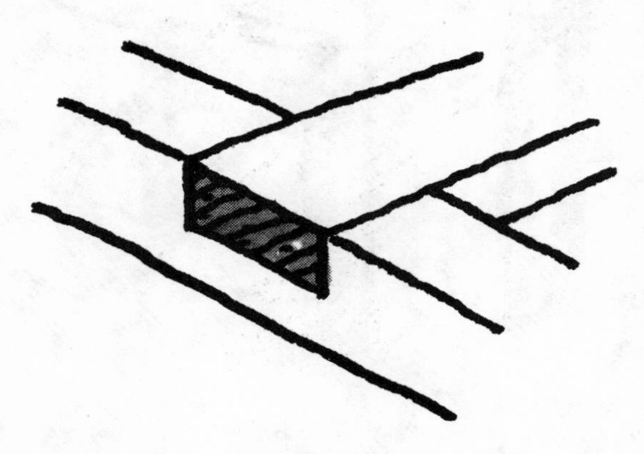

Full lap

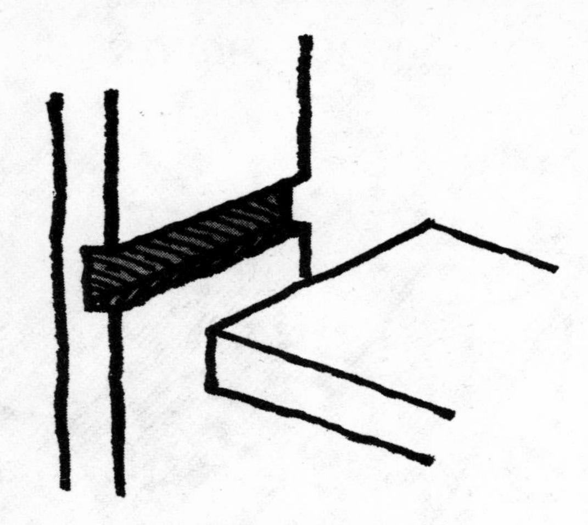

Through housing

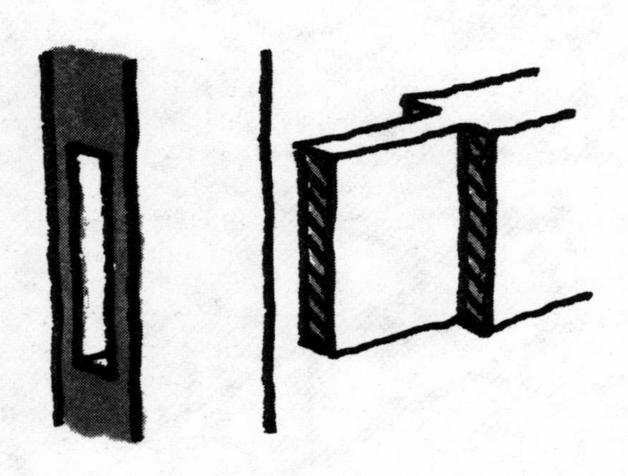

Mortise and tenon

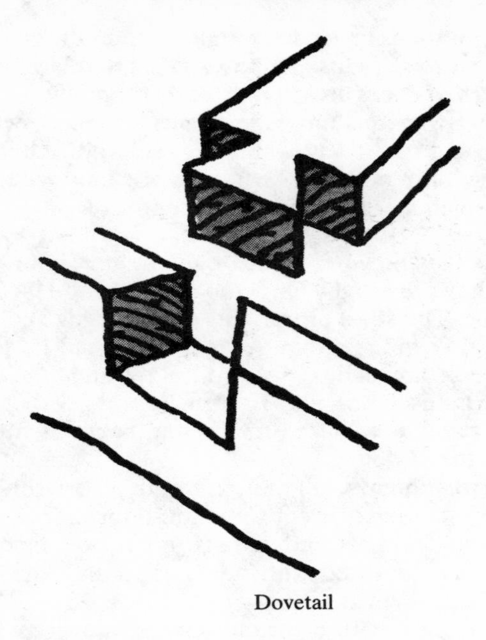

Dovetail

DOORS

Internal doors range from paper honeycombs covered with hardboard which a determined toddler could put his bootee through to panelled hardwood capable of stopping an Exocet, and the range of prices reflects the great variation in quality. Cheaper than solid hardwood doors but similar in appearance are those that consist of a core of medium density fibreboard faced with a hardwood veneer.

Many **panelled doors**, both softwood and hardwood, were hardboarded over during the national obsession with flush-fitting surfaces after the last war. If a door seems heavy for its size, check for nail heads around the edges and try levering a corner away if you are not too concerned about causing damage. If there is a panelled gem underneath, the door can be taken to the local caustic-bath practitioner to be stripped and then painted or stained to taste. DIY vandals who took the job seriously tended to glue wood on the panels to support the hardboard and tore off the mouldings. Where this has been done the door will have to be left well alone or replaced.

If work on the house is being done under a grant the council may insist on one or more self-closing **fire-doors**, particularly if a flat is involved. **Concertina doors** are often used as room dividers. These are made of long thin sections, sometimes panelled, which are hinged together and fold away when not required. Alternatively **sliding doors** which run on a track can be used. **Louvred doors** are made of slats which permit ventilation, and are often used on built-in wardrobes.

External doors may now be plastic or aluminium, but if they are panelled wood they are usually hardwood or softwood faced with a hardwood veneer. The **stiles** or uprights on each side should be at least 100 mm (4 in) wide so that security locks can be installed. Flush external doors are made of waterproof ply and have a central block of wood to hold a letter box. To form a good weather-seal the doors must be rebated to fit over a **water bar** and fitted with **weatherboard** at the bottom.

Wooden **French windows** will look 'right' in a period house but uPVC and aluminium have swept the patio-door market because they keep out the draughts and require no maintenance. Patio doors should always be fitted with safety glass and high-security locks as burglars like them as well.

Wooden doors come with protruding stiles known as **horns** to protect them and these should be cut off before the door is fitted. **Hinges** are usually placed 150 mm (6 in) from the top and 230 mm (9 in) from the bottom. If the door is very heavy or an external one a third hinge is placed in the centre. Allow 3 mm (⅛ in) clearance at the top and on the lock side and 6 mm (¼ in) at the bottom. Use wedges to keep the door off the floor while fitting it, and recess the hinges into both the door and the frame by judicious use of the chisel.

Where a door sticks on a new carpet, replacing the regular butt hinges with rising butt hinges will lift it over. A door that sticks in the frame will need planing off, but it is not always obvious exactly where the problem lies. Before removing the door slide a piece of paper down the gap between door and frame and mark where it meets an obstruction. Alternatively, chalk the edge of the door and then look for the places on the frame where the chalk has rubbed off. If the door is binding on the hinge stile, the hinges may have been recessed too deeply and should be packed out with cardboard. If the hinges become loose, repack the holes with wood or use longer screws — but beware of using screws of a larger diameter with heads that will stand out of the hinge and prevent the door from closing easily. When a frame becomes loose, drill through into the masonry, push a plastic plug down the hole and screw through.

WINDOWS

Despite the popularity of new materials the vast majority of window frames are still made from wood. A softwood ready-made window is the cheapest around and its insulation properties are excellent. The drawbacks are the fact that it requires regular maintenance in the form of painting and the threat of rot. Make sure the frame has been pressure impregnated with preservative and buy a hardwood frame if your budget will stretch to it — it will last longer whether stained and varnished or painted.

Sash windows used to be common, but their tendency to rattle and stick and the heart-stopping crash of the counterweight when the sash cord suddenly parted led many householders to replace them with **casement windows** with panes that open outwards. The result has often ruined the appearance of a Georgian facade. However, sash windows are now available again in wood or even aluminium and spring balances have replaced the cords and weights.

Aluminium windows are available in anodized or acrylic finishes as well as the natural silvery-grey. Maintenance requirements are limited to the occasional wash with soap and water, but the anodized finish can sometimes become pitted as a result of corrosion. Aluminium is a very poor insulation material and the windows should be fitted with a **thermal break** or insulator inside the frame. A combined aluminium and uPVC frame also helps solve the insulation problem.

uPVC windows need no maintenance and have excellent insulation properties. The only drawback is uPVC's vulnerability to scratches and direct heat.

Steel windows were introduced between the wars and are rarely used as replacements. Poor insulation, condensation problems and rust that defies even regular painting have resulted in their being quite properly unloved.

Standard **double-glazing** units need an extra-large rebate in the window frame to hold them. Where the rebate is small, stepped-edge units with one pane larger than the other can be used. Safety glass should be used in glass doors or windows near the bath, at the foot of stairs and in other places where a falling person might be expected to land. **Toughened** or **annealed** glass shatters into harmless tiny fragments instead of the usual razor-sharp daggers. **Laminated** glass has one or more layers of a plastic called polyvinyl butyral (PVB) sandwiched in it and under impact it will craze but not break. A PVB layer also improves sound insulation, although heat insulation is hardly affected.

When replacing a window you may be lucky and find that the old one is a standard size and you can buy a new one ready-made. If not, get one made to the dimensions of the old one. Remove the glass of the old window and then the frame, which will be screwed or nailed into the wall at each side or held with brackets inserted into the mortar. It is often easier to saw up the old frame as it stands rather than remove it in one piece. Minimize damage to the plaster and decoration inside the room by heavily scoring round the inside edge of the frame so it comes away cleanly. Remove the old plugs from the wall and replace them with new ones to take the screws. Mark and drill holes in the frame for the screws, which should be zinc coated. Stand the frame in the window opening. It should have a clearance of about 6 mm (¼ in) all the way round. Screw the frame to the wall using packing pieces to make sure it is not pulled over to one side and fill the gaps round the edge with mastic.

STUD WALLS

A stud wall is a timber-framed non-load-bearing plasterboard wall used to create rooms or subdivide them. The frame is usually constructed out of 75-mm-by-50-mm (3-in-by-2-in) timber. First mark out the position on the floor and mark a corresponding line on the ceiling using a plumb-line to make sure they match. Ideally the top piece or **head** will run across the ceiling joists and can be fixed to them. If it runs parallel to the joists, either make sure it runs underneath one or install pieces of bridging timber between the joists. The head and the floor piece or **sole plate** should be cut and the positions of the vertical timbers of the wall, called **studs**, should be marked at 61-cm (2-ft) centres to make it easy to fix the plasterboard.

A good craftsperson will now saw and chisel out housing joints for the studs to sit in in the head and sole plate, but many ordinary mortals tend not to bother. Screw the head and sole plate in position

STUD WALL CONSTRUCTION

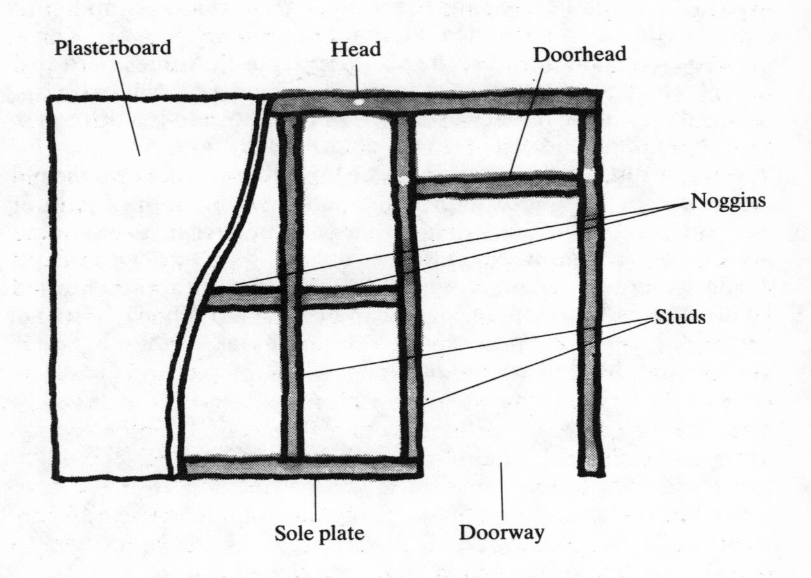

(watching out for water pipes or electricity cables) and cut the studs to length. Whether they are seated in housing joints or not they should be **skew nailed**, in other words nailed at an angle, into the plate and the head. Alternatively they can be drilled and screwed.

The horizontal pieces, called **noggins**, should now be cut and skew nailed to the studs at 122-cm (4-ft) centres. Extra noggins will have to be inserted to take the screws from wash-basins, cupboards and so on. Now is also the time to run in power sockets and water and central-heating pipes. The plasterboard should be cut 12 mm (½ in) shorter than the full height of the partition and pressed tight against the ceiling before it is nailed. The gap will be covered later by the skirting board. No house yet built has walls that are at true right angles to the floor and the board will have to be **scribed** before it is cut so that it matches the eccentricities of the wall. Set the first board as close to the wall as possible and run the point of a pair of compasses down the wall while the pencil traces each bulge and incline on to the board. At the other end set the last board face to face with the penultimate one and cut a 122-cm (4-ft) length of timber. While a helper runs the lath slowly down the wall hold a pencil to the other end to mark the board.

If you intend to decorate the wall directly use Gyproc board with a tapered edge fixed with the ivory face outwards. Nail with galvanized plasterboard nails every 150 mm (6 in), driving them in so that they dimple the surface of the board. Fill the joints between the boards in this way: apply a band of joint-filler with an applicator which can be bought or improvised and press a length of jointing tape on top. Follow this with another band of filler that completely fills the tapered joint. Make sure it finishes flush and wipe off the surplus filler with a damp sponge. After this has set apply a layer of joint finish and feather the edges with the sponge. When it is dry put on another coat of finish in a broad band, feather the edges and complete with a final coat of finish.

8

KEEPING WARM

'The Frost severer than ever in the night as it even froze the Chamber Pots under the Beds.'
(Parson Woodforde's diary entry for 28 February 1785)

The Romans survived during their stay in Britain by drinking wine and installing underfloor ducted hot-air central heating. The natives were both hardy and ignorant, and therefore scornful of such fancy foreign ways. Consequently, shivering was part of being British for the next 1,500 years or so. Only since the last war has central heating come to be regarded as a necessity rather than an indulgence, and anyone born before the sixties can remember the family huddled round a sullen grate of wet slack in the living-room and permafrost in the bathroom. Thankfully, high standards of insulation and a host of heating techniques are putting an end to all that.

CENTRAL HEATING

Like Conservative politicians and abrasive paper, central heating comes wet and dry. Wet systems use water heated in a boiler to carry warmth about the house, releasing it through radiators. Dry systems rely on directly heating air to warm the house. There is no ideal heating system. Each has advantages and disadvantages and what is appropriate for one house may be inappropriate for another. When ordering a central heating system:

- Get estimates from a number of firms and compare their designs and prices.
- Be wary of firms that concentrate on just one product and always try at least one dealer who does not specialize in any particular type of heating.
- Insist on a detailed account of what you're getting. This should set out the standards and regulations to which the work is being carried out, the size and make of the boiler and where it will be sited, the temperature level that the design is based on (usually 21° C inside when it is −1° C outside), the type of radiators, their rating and where they will go, and whether any insulation is included in the price.

Wet systems: Water is heated in the boiler, pumped round a system of radiators and then returned to the boiler to be reheated. The usual system, known as **small bore** in contrast to the systems with large iron pipes once common, can be **single-pipe** or **two-pipe**.

In single-pipe systems one copper pipe takes the hot water to and

SINGLE-, TWO-PIPE AND MICROBORE HEATING SYSTEMS

Single-pipe heating system

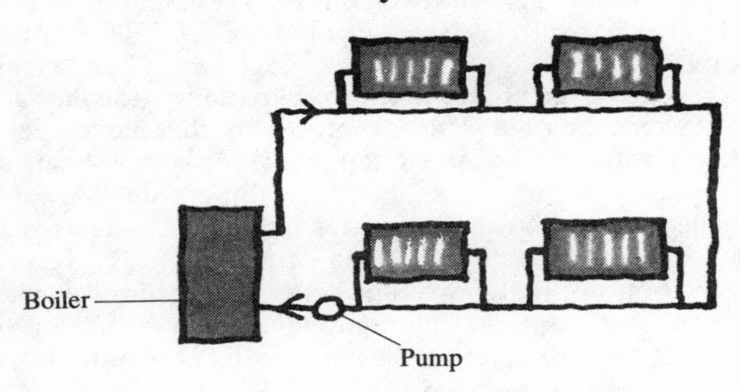

Two-pipe heating system

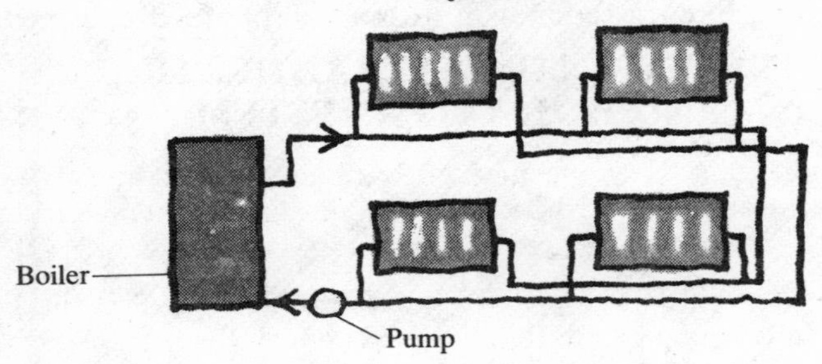

Microbore heating system

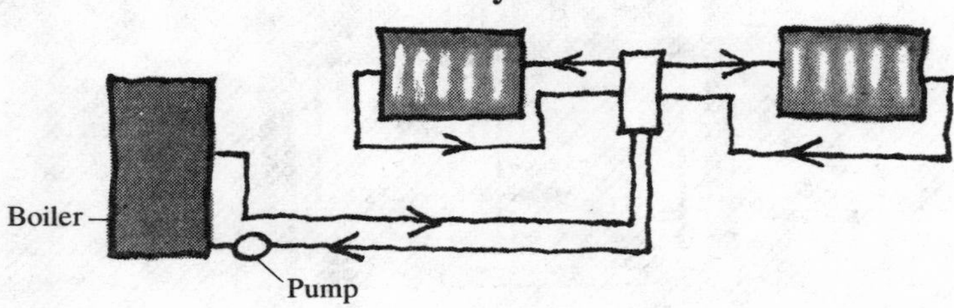

from each radiator in turn, first upstairs and then downstairs, and finally back to the boiler. At each radiator the water loses heat so the radiators at the end of the system will not be as warm as those at the start.

The two-pipe system helps to overcome this problem. One pipe still takes the hot water to each radiator but the cooled water that comes out of the other end of the radiator is collected by a second pipe which returns to the boiler. In technical parlance, the **flow** and the **return** are kept separate. The advantages are that the temperature of the hot water is maintained and the whole system heats up much more quickly. A further benefit is the neatness of the installation. In single-pipe fittings the hot water enters the radiator near the top and descends under the action of gravity to the return, which is at the bottom. In the two-pipe system the return valve lets the water only trickle out at a rate that makes the best use of the heat and as a result both pipes can be connected at the bottom and even in some cases at the same point.

Microbore systems use 6-mm, 8-mm or 10-mm pipe instead of the 15-mm pipe that single- and two-pipe systems employ. Instead of the pipe going to each radiator in turn a microbore circuit feeds

CONVENTIONAL CENTRAL HEATING AND HOT-WATER SYSTEM

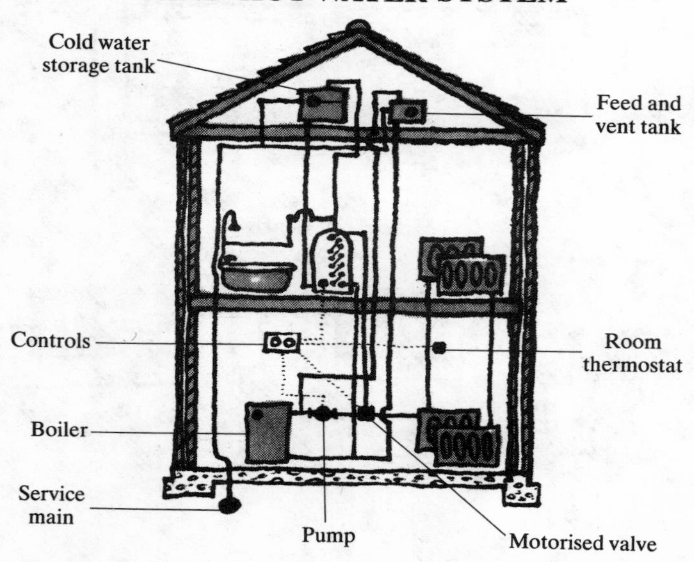

each from a central distribution point called a **manifold**.

A wet system in which water is heated by the boiler will be linked to the domestic hot-water suply. The boiler will supply hot water not only to the radiators but also to the hot-water storage cistern. In Britain the hot-water system is known as an **open system** because the boiler and the hot-water cylinder are fed and vented by means of an open storage tank in the loft (see Chapter Five).

Sealed systems are now being accepted in Britain. These dispense with the cold-water storage and venting arrangements. The boiler takes cold water from the mains, heats it and stores it in a pressurized cylinder. In the open system overheated water can escape up the vent pipe. In the sealed system the expansion is taken up by a pressure vessel containing an inert gas such as nitrogen. Because of the problems of greater pressure with the sealed systems manufacturers are going to some trouble to design their products with all the safety devices correctly installed. However, it is still worth making sure that the plumber you employ to install such a system has experience of them or has been on a training course of the kind run by at least one major manufacturer.

SEALED CENTRAL HEATING AND HOT-WATER SYSTEM

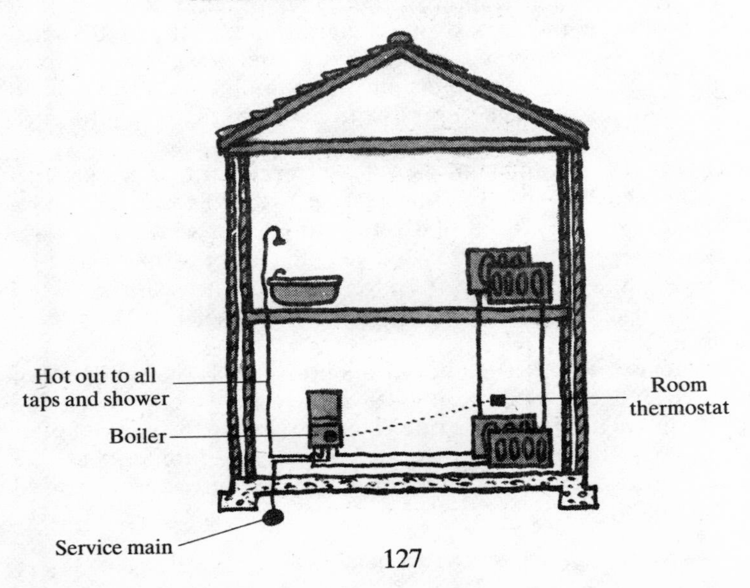

★ **Pumps**: Inconspicuous, quiet and hard-working, the pump is the heart of the wet heating system, and like all hearts it will be taken for granted until it finally stops. It can be fitted in either the return or the flow pipes, either pushing or sucking the water round the system. A modern pump can work for years without needing attention or causing problems, but it should have a gate valve on the inlet and the outlet so that it can be serviced without the system's having to be drained. If a pump is replaced make sure that the new one gives the correct rate of flow and that the arrow indicating the flow direction is pointing the same way as before. The pump may drive only the central-heating water while the ordinary hot water rises from boiler to storage cylinder under the action of gravity, or both circulations may be pumped.

★ **Radiators**: Radiators are rated in BTUs (British Thermal Units). A BTU measures the quantity of heat that will raise the temperature of one pound weight of water by 10° F. To calculate the size of radiator required very complicated calculations can be done involving the space to be heated, the degree of insulation, ventilation and so on. But most friendly plumbers' merchants will do this for you.

The most common radiator is the **panel** kind which can be a single or double panel thick depending on the heat output required. A further development to improve output has been the addition of convector fins on the back. Panel radiators are usually sited underneath windows where they counteract the cold down-draught from the glass, but this is less important where double glazing has been installed and the householder is free to put the radiators in the most convenient spot.

Radiators have either an air-release screw, which is loosened with a special key to allow the system to be bled of air, or an automatic air vent. Those that refuse to get hot while others are working properly are likely to need bleeding to get rid of the air that is stopping the hot water from getting in. The worst affected radiator is usually the highest one, because all the air in the system has risen to it.

If a radiator isn't getting hot at the bottom it is probably full of corrosive sludge caused by air getting into the system and reacting with the metal to form iron oxide. This can clog up the pump, boiler and valves and ultimately cause leaks. Chemical inhibitors can be added to the system and if air is getting in the cause must be traced and remedied.

Each radiator should have two valves fitted so that the panel can be removed if necessary without the system's being drained. One of the valves should be of the **wheelhead** type and is used to turn the radiator on and off. The other should be of the **lockshield** type which is turned with a special key and is used for **balancing** the system after installation. A pair of clip-on thermometers is put on the flow and return pipes of each radiator and the lockshield valves are manipulated until all the radiators reach the same temperature. The radiators nearest the pump will need their lockshield valves to be only slightly open, while the valves on those furthest away will be opened wide.

Skirting radiators are fitted in place of the skirting boards and consist of metal fins with a tube through the middle. The hot air enters the room through a damper which regulates the flow. **Convector** radiators use an electric fan to blow hot air past a heat-exchanger into the room. They take up much less space than panel radiators but the noise of the fan can be irritating.

Dry systems: The classic dry system works by means of **ducted hot air**, the method the Romans hit upon. A boiler heats the air which is then distributed about the house through a series of ducts in the walls and under the floors. The design of the system is critical to its success and dry systems of this type are difficult to install except during the construction of a house. They work best in houses that have highly insulated walls and the duct grilles must be kept clear of any obstruction; cats are often found against them, keeping themselves warm while their owners freeze.

Underfloor electric heating has got a bad press as a result of people finding their home is an oven run at vast expense while the sun is blazing through the windows. The principle is that of using elements in the floor which turn the floor into a single giant storage heater. But once it's hot there is no way of turning it off, and in a fickle climate such as Britain's such inflexibility is particularly inconvenient. Another problem is that the thicker your carpet the less easily the heat can rise, and you may find you have insulated the room from the heating source.

Electric ceiling heating is usually installed in conjunction with underfloor heating. This also has elements which get hot but it is not a storage system.

The **storage heater** is a great advance on the storage floor. The heaters are wired to the Economy 7 meter which will be installed by the electricity board. These then take power at a cheap rate for seven hours during the period of low demand in the night and use it to create heat which is emitted through the day. One of the problems used to be that the heaters burned all day while no one was home and by the time evening came when the family returned and temperatures fell it was going cold. Improved insulation in a house helps to combat this, and modern storage heaters also have controls which restrict the emission of heat more efficiently. If the heat isn't needed at all then it stays inside the unit to provide the basis of the next day's supply. Experts recommend the use of convector heaters or electric fires in addition to provide 'top-up' heat when it is needed.

Storage heaters are cheaper to install than most other systems and the modern generation of heaters are also much less bulky than their forebears. Having an Economy 7 meter also allows you to take advantage of the cheap electricity by running your washing machine, dish-washer and any other gadget at night.

Boilers: These may be run on gas, oil, electricity or solid fuel.

⋆ **Gas** boilers come in three different forms: the **back boiler** to a gas fire mounted in the fireplace, the **free-standing** boiler and the **wall-mounted** boiler. The back boiler model will make use of an existing flue to get rid of waste gases, but the other two can be either **conventionally flued** or **room sealed** with a **balanced flue** which is taken through the brickwork to an unobtrusive grille outside.

Silent running, no fuel to order, carry or store, no lighting procedure or smells, highly competitive running costs — these are the advantages that have made gas boilers so popular. They are completely safe, being fitted with a device that prevents gas from being released unless the pilot light has been lit and the boiler is fully operational.

Sealed-system **combi boilers** heat the cold water directly from the mains and don't need a separate feed and expansion tank. However, the flow rate is limited and where demand may be large a storage vessel is required to meet it. When the central heating isn't required in the summer the combi boiler acts as a **multipoint heater**, instantly heating water for whichever hot tap is in use.

Houses that are unable to have a mains gas supply can use **LPG (Liquified Petroleum Gas)** which is supplied to a tank in the garden. This is regularly topped up by a tanker. There are regulations stipulating that the tank is a minimum distance from the house and houses with small gardens may lack sufficient space. In this case gas in metal cylinders can be used. LPG boilers look and work like ordinary gas boilers but they are not interchangeable.

⋆ **Oil** boilers tend to be more expensive than gas ones and noisier. As a result, many are banished to cellars and outbuildings. However, the modern **pressure jet** type are much quieter than the older **wallflame** models. Oil boilers are usually floor mounted but some models can be wall-hung with a balanced flue. The boilers are sturdy and should have a long life but they will require an annual service to be kept in peak condition.

The oil is stored in a nearby tank and this can be filled whenever is most convenient for the householder, i.e. when there's some spare cash about. Many oil companies offer a monthly payment system similar to those available to gas and electricity users, and by ordering in the summer when demand is low a substantial discount can usually be claimed.

The major problem with oil is the fluctuating price. Like any major world commodity oil is subject to the interference of wars and international tension. At the time of writing it is one of the cheapest fuels following years when it was about the most expensive. Britain has benefited from having its own supplies of both oil and gas but these are now diminishing and it is a matter for speculation what effect this will have on prices in the future.

⋆ **Electricity** can also be used to run a wet central-heating system by means of an Economy 7 boiler which uses cheap-rate electricity. This boiler can be either the solid-core type, which transfers heat to water via a heat-exchanger, or the hot-water storage type, which acts rather like a super immersion heater and holds the water until it is needed. The stored hot water is used during the day and reheated at night. It can be given a boost during the day but then the electricity costs the full price.

Economy 7 boilers can heat domestic hot water as well, or a conventional immersion heater can be used. Immersion heaters may have one element inserted vertically in the tank or two smaller ones inserted in the side. Dual elements save money by allowing just the top of the cylinder to be heated if only a small quantity of hot water is required. The whole tank is heated by the lower element which can be connected to the Economy 7 meter.

⋆ **Solid-fuel** boilers and open fires were largely ousted as means of heating homes by the lower cost and greater convenience of gas and electricity. These newcomers started and stopped at the touch of a switch, didn't need Scout-like skills with sticks and paper to get them going, and never required you to go out in a snowstorm at night to fill the coal-bucket. However, the solid-fuel boffins have fought back with hopper-fed models that need feeding only every few days or even less than once a week. Electric fans and thermostatic dampers give greater control, and ash can be removed automatically. Modern self-contained solid-fuel boilers resemble the floor-mounted gas models and can be used in kitchens and basements where they will give no direct heat to the room.

Advances in fuel and fire technology mean that open grates with back boilers can not only provide hot water for a house but also run several radiators. Even more efficient are stoves with doors or **room-heaters** such as the cast-iron log-burning stoves that are becoming increasingly popular. Most will burn a variety of fuels and apart from heating the room will run a reasonably sized central-heating system.

Aga or Rayburn-style cooker/stoves make sense in big, draughty kitchens as they heat the room, provide a lot of hot water and cook the dinner all at the same time. The problem with the traditional solid-fuel model is that its constant heat becomes uncomfortable in hot weather. However, more controllable gas- and oil-fired versions are now also produced.

A solid-fuel system will need a dry store big enough to take a couple of tons of coal or smokeless fuel. An annual visit by the chimney sweep is also necessary, although there are chemicals that can be put on a fire to clean the flue.

Heating controls: A **thermostat** is a kind of switch operated automatically when a pre-determined temperature is reached. Immersion heaters have thermostats which cut them out to stop the water boiling. Central-heating boilers are often controlled by a single **room thermostat**. The disadvantage with this is that the temperature of the whole house is dependent on how hot or cold that particular room is. Thus if the room in which the thermostat is located has another source of heating, such as an open fire, the radiators throughout the house will switch off even though the other rooms are freezing. Alternatively the whole house may be heated at unnecessary expense, when only a couple of rooms actually need to be.

The answer is to have a **thermostatic radiator valve (TRV)** on each radiator, each set to whatever temperature is required in that room. If a new system is being installed it makes economic sense to use TRVs, but they may be expensive to use on an old system as the pipes could be of a different dimension. A plumbers' merchant will tell you whether the valves correspond if you can describe the make or size of your old ones.

Thermostatic valves work by keeping the hot water out of a radiator or letting it in depending on the room's temperature. But they can't tell the boiler to switch off as the room thermostat does. A recent innovation on the domestic market is a controller which prevents wasteful overheating by the boiler. It senses the outdoor temperature and works out just how much heat the boiler needs to put out to allow the thermostatic valves to keep the house at the pre-set temperature.

Apart from immersion heater thermostats, hot-water cylinders can have a thermostat to cut off the hot-water supply from the boiler when the water in the cylinder reaches a satisfactory temperature. The boiler will heat water to, say, 80°C when hot tap water need be only 60°C. This device is particularly helpful in preventing the high temperatures in the hot-water system that encourage the formation of scale. Perhaps even more usefully, it prevents the unwary being scalded when they get into the bath.

A **frost thermostat** will turn a boiler on when the temperature nears freezing. This will prevent an outhouse boiler from freezing solid if it is left for a few days while the family hit the ski slopes.

The circulation of water can be controlled by **motorized valves** as well as by thermostats. These are operated by electricity to allow hot water to flow to the central-heating or the hot-water system, or both. Motorized valves allow **zone control** which permits different temperature settings for different areas of the house.

Overall command of the central-heating system is achieved via the **timer** and the **programmer**. These used to be simple electromechanical devices combining a clock and switches. Now they have been thoroughly microchipped which has resulted in push buttons, digital displays and a flexibility that allows a different programme for every day.

ALTERNATIVE HEATING

In a solar heating system flat plate **collectors** are mounted on the roof, facing south if possible. A heat-transfer liquid is warmed as it goes through the collector and then circulates to an indirect cylinder where it heats the water surrounding the calorifier. Solar heating is really designed to supplement other water-heating methods. The installation cost is high and the system is not generally regarded as cost effective at present.

Like solar panels, heat pumps appear to be on a par with scientific chimeras such as perpetual motion and anti-gravity machines in that they give you something for nothing. They work like a fridge in that they extract heat, but instead of throwing it out of the back they use it to warm the domestic water. They can make gains from a very small temperature difference and thus outside air or, less usually, a stretch of water is the source of heat. Again as in the case of solar heating, the hitch is the initial cost of installing the system when weighed against the financial gains. But both systems are likely to grow in popularity as technology improves and fuel costs rise.

FIRES AND FLUES

By the end of the sixties the fires were going out all over Europe as people abandoned dirty and demanding open grates, covered the flue opening with hardboard and wallpaper and stuck a gas or electric fire in front of it. Since then the hardboard has steadily been coming off again as householders, driven no doubt by some primeval itch, choose to roast their toes in front of flames. The difference is that in the sixties the fire was still the main source of heat in many houses, whereas now that efficient central heating is commonplace the open fire or stove is often more of an ornament. However, it can also be a very practical ornament that heats water and feeds radiators.

The chimney: Much mystic nonsense is talked about the construction of an efficient flue, and although builders sometimes make a hash of it there is really no excuse. The principles are quite simple.

The hot air inside a chimney is less dense than the cold air outside. This means that the pressure is lower inside the flue and the air is drawn upwards. The rules are:

- The taller and straighter the flue the better it will work. In apparent defiance of this the flues in Victorian chimneys often have one or more dog-legs to bring them together in a single chimney stack and they still work perfectly well. Science dictates, though, that the bend should be at an angle not less than 45° from the horizontal and something nearer 60° is better.
- A well-insulated chimney will also work better than a chilly one because the air is kept hotter, which encourages it to rise more quickly.
- The size of the fireplace opening must not be more than eight times the area of a cross section of the flue, or the smoke and gas may cool in the fireplace area before it is drawn upwards and will fall back into the room.
- The flue should be smooth internally so that turbulence in the air flow is avoided. Also, there should be no nooks or steps in the fireplace opening for smoke to cool under. To avoid this a **gather** is used to funnel the air smoothly from the fireplace opening into the flue. The narrowing creates a venturi effect by forcing the hot gases to accelerate as they pass through.
- The chimney stack must not finish lower than the highest point of the house (usually the ridge), to avoid down-draught problems.

A malfunctioning chimney can quickly turn the living-room into something resembling a kipper-curing shed. Flues are prone to a number of ailments all of which can be classed as either **up-draught** problems or **down-draught** problems.

Where an old flue is being brought back into use the first thing to check is the up-draught. Light a piece of paper in the grate and check that the flame is drawn upwards. If it isn't, call in the sweep to make sure the flue isn't obstructed by soot. The sweep's brush may also dislodge any loose rubble that has accumulated. Occasionally flues may become solidly blocked, perhaps by a collapse of the **feathering**, the brickwork separating one flue from another inside the chimney breast. If this is the case, a heavy round weight on a chain dropped from the top of the stack may clear it, but this may also cause more damage to the feathering. In any case this brickwork will need to be reconstructed before the flue will work properly, so the best option is probably to open up the chimney breast at the point where the blockage has occurred.

If the fireplace is smoking and the flue is clear, check that double glazing and draught-proofing aren't robbing the fire of the air it needs to replace that going up the chimney. If the fire works only with the door or window open then a **ventilator grille** is needed. The best spot for this is probably over the door as this avoids causing draughts round the feet and pulling cold air from outside into the house.

Large fireplace openings may be too big for the size of flue. Check this using the 8:1 formula. If the throat itself is too large, install a **throat-restrictor**, a metal unit which sits on top of the fireback and allows the size of the throat to be varied by means of a lever. If the throat is very rough it should be rendered to provide a smooth funnel into the flue.

Problems caused by oversized openings, particularly those higher than 56 cm (22 in), can sometimes be cured with a **hood**. Experiment with different sizes and shapes in cardboard before ordering one in sheet metal. Special extractor fans can be placed in the flue to draw smoke up when it is reluctant to rise of its own accord.

Where a stove is smoking check that the horizontal flue outlet hasn't been installed so far back in the vertical flue that the escape of gases is being restricted. There ought to be a gap of at least 10 cm (4 in). Cold air leaking in through soot doors and register plates will also cause smoking.

A poor up-draught may also be caused at the other end of the flue because a tapering chimney pot or one narrower than the flue has been put on and is restricting the flow of gases. Replace it with a straight-sided one that matches the dimensions of the flue.

A flue may also be affected by down-draught. As the wind presses on the roof it creates high pressure which opposes the rise of air from the stack. Meanwhile the other side of the house will be in a low-pressure area and this will help draw air down the flue. Even where a chimney is a proper height it can still be affected by occasional turbulence caused by high trees or buildings nearby. A **cowl** is the usual answer to this and there is a staggering variety of these devices which either sit on the pot or replace it.

If the fire appears to be working properly but smoke is making its way into other parts of the house it indicates that the chimney needs **relining**. It is not uncommon when old flues are used for the first time in many years to find there is a smell of smoke upstairs. In bad cases bedrooms can become uninhabitable and furniture and carpets may be stained by smoke emerging through floor spaces and round window frames.

What has happened is that many years' exposure to soot has corroded the soft lime mortar holding the bricks of the feathering. Smoke makes its way into other flues and then into the wall cavity if there is one. From there it will emerge into rooms through any opening it finds. There are three basic ways of relining a chimney:

- Covering the leaky internal surface with a layer of **liquid cement**. This solution is widely and irreverently known as the rubber sausage method. What is essentially a long rubber balloon is inserted in the chimney and inflated. This then acts as a former for the liquid cement which is pumped up to the top of the house and poured around it. When the cement sets the balloon is withdrawn. Where there are bends in the chimney, holes must be made, from either inside or outside the house, and the balloon supported so that it remains central in the flue.

  Contractors using this method should, if they are competent, first carefully survey the chimney and carry out a smoke test to make sure that there are no large holes requiring filling before work begins. Cowboy operators have been known to keep pouring cement into a sieve-like flue until it starts coming out of the window frames. In one regularly cited horror story it flowed into next door's flue and filled the living-room. When properly done, however, this method provides an efficient and long-lasting cure.

- Building a **chimney within a chimney** using liner pipes. The traditional answer to relining was to open up the whole chimney breast and cement a lot of clay pipes together to form a new flue. The modern version of these pipes are pumice-based tubes which withstand high temperatures and chimney fires far better than clay. Where a chimney is straight the tubes can be fed in one at a time from the top and linked together with steel collars as they are lowered; this avoids the need to open up the chimney breast. Holes in walls are unavoidable, though, if the flue bends, as angled joints will have to be made at these points. The tubes are surrounded by pebbles of expanded clay held together with a little cement. This holds the flue in place and provides excellent insulation, making a more efficient flue.

- Installing a **flexible stainless-steel tube** within the old flue. Flexible double-skinned steel liners have been in use for many years in France and Canada and provide the simplest relining method. The tube is merely fed down the chimney and around bends — as long as they are not more than 45° from the vertical. The saving on labour, however, is lost to some extent on the high cost of the tube, and its guaranteed life of 10 years is shorter than the length of time one would expect the other methods to last.

A flue that is too narrow to take liners and too irregular or unsound for cement lining need not necessarily be reconstructed. The Danish company Iso-Kearn, makers of pumice liners, have devised a **mechanical reamer** which will cut its way down the chimney and widen it enough to allow liners to be installed.

The fireplace: Uncovering an old fireplace is no problem unless a gas fire and boiler have been installed in the opening. If this is the case they should be dismantled by experts and a new site found for a boiler. If the opening has been bricked or boarded up a hollow sound should reveal where to start with hammer and chisel. The work should be done carefully so as not to damage an old fireback that may be still usable.

In terraces or semis where the fireplaces in adjoining houses are placed back to back there is also the danger of bursting through into next door, and more than one builder has wound up shaking hands with strangers after falling into their living-room in a cloud of brick and plaster dust. After opening up the fireplace, check the draught with a piece of lighted paper or with smoke pellets lit in the grate. The case is recorded of an enthusiastic convert to open fires who created a monumental fireplace in stone before discovering that the entire chimney had been removed from the house from bedroom-floor level. It is more likely, if the chimney hasn't been used for some time, that it has simply been capped to keep out the rain. Ensure that the capping is removed from the right flue. One couple spent £800 on having a reopened chimney relined because it smoked badly before discovering they had uncapped the wrong flue.

FIREPLACE CONSTRUCTION

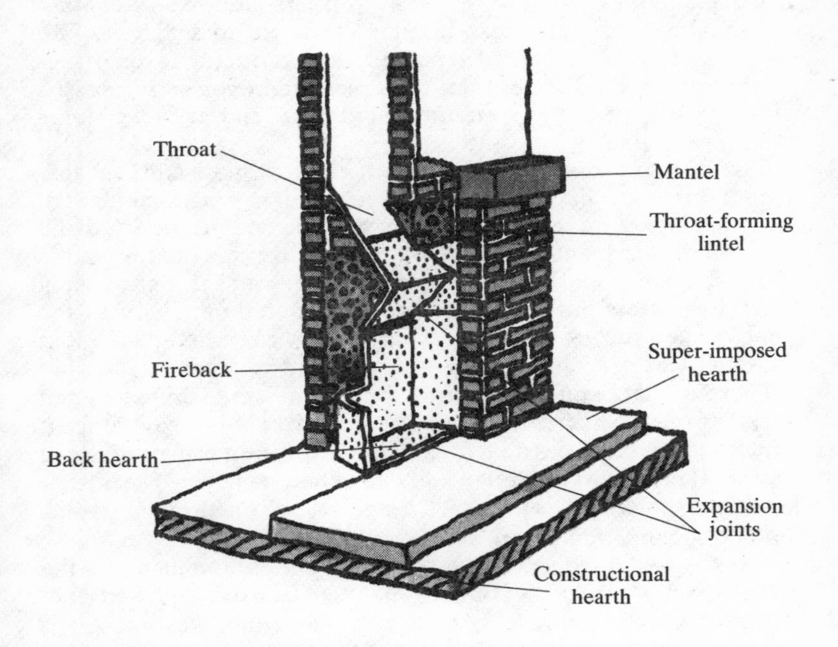

If you are lucky the chimney will draw and the hearth will still be in place. If there is no hearth one will have to be made. A **constructional hearth** is normally a slab of concrete 125 mm (5 in) thick, which must extend not less than 51 mm (20 in) in front of the chimney breast and at least 150 mm (6 in) each side of the opening. This can be bought from a builders' merchant or made on site. The hearth will need to be supported below floor level and consent will be needed from the local building inspector before the work begins. If the floor is already solid it may qualify as a constructional hearth. On top of a constructional hearth goes the **superimposed hearth** which should be made out of quarry tiles, slate, marble or any other non-combustible material.

It is a truism that one generation's junk is the prized possession of the next. **Fire surrounds** that were being ripped out and dumped 20 years ago are now fetching hundreds of pounds in antique shops. The demand for wood, tiled and cast-iron surrounds is so great that high-quality reproductions are being produced to satisfy it. Fire surrounds are normally held in place by screws or nails through lugs on the top or sides. These are then plastered over and it can be tricky trying to release an unwanted surround without doing considerable damage.

Cast-iron surrounds often come with a built-in grate and **fireback**. Where this is absent or where a fireplace is being constructed out of stone or slate, a fire-clay back will have to be bought, inserted and fixed with fire cement. The back is moulded to guide out the smoke and gases. This should be used in conjunction with a throat-forming **lintel**, a concrete lintel with the back chamfered parallel with the slope of the fireback to form a **throat**. The throat should be about 100 mm (4 in) deep and the same width as the fire opening.

There is a large number of firms who install stone fireplaces and many offer kits which can be easily assembled by the inexperienced. However, it is quite possible for anyone with minimal experience of stone and brickwork to design and make their own. The best idea is to inspect showrooms where such fireplaces are on display and pick their designers' brains quite shamelessly.

The simplest open fire is the traditional grate standing under the flue. The only form of air control is likely to be a damper in front of the ash-pan. More efficient is the underfloor draught fire. Air is ducted under the floorboards or, if the floor is solid, through a pipe connected to an air-brick on the outside wall. Back or wrap-around boilers are usually available for these types of fire. Stoves keep the fire enclosed behind doors and are much more efficient water-heaters. Glass-fronted stoves are a distinctively British device, resulting from our need to be able to see the fire that is warming us. Wood-burning stoves usually have cast-iron doors and despite their name most will burn either wood or solid fuel. In towns fires and room-heaters will have to run on smokeless fuel to meet the requirements of the Clean Air Acts, but some room-heaters are designed to burn ordinary coal without breaking the regulations.

Although houses are once again being built with chimneys many constructed over the last 30 years don't have one. It is possible to add a chimney to the house using brick, stone, breeze block or thermal load-bearing blocks. A masonry chimney can easily weigh four tons and must be built off similar foundations to the house whether it is constructed inside or outside. Pre-fabricated chimneys make construction much simpler and these fall into three categories:

- Twin-wall insulated metal.
- Ceramic-lined metal.
- Pre-cast blocks with an insulated liner.

The metal tubes are easy to assemble and take up little room, and the stove pipe look may be attractive in the right circumstances. The pre-cast blocks are free-standing although they are usually rebated into the building. They are quicker to assemble than masonry chimneys and can be rendered, plastered, or clad in brick or stone to match the surrounding finish. Note that the regulations concerning chimney construction are very detailed and vary from area to area, so a visit from the building inspector to your premises is a must.

INSULATION

The air that is so expensively heated inside the house is constantly sneaking out through walls, windows and roofs. Good insulation can cut the escape rate by up to 50 per cent.

Walls: The air barrier in a cavity wall is sufficient to restrict heat loss, but it is more effective to fill this cavity with insulation material. The usual method is to drill holes in the wall and blow in **urea formaldehyde (UF) foam**, **polystyrene pellets** or **mineral fibres**.

Some controversy has surrounded the use of UF foam and it seems that some people suffer irritation to eyes and throat in its presence. An investigation by the Building Research Establishment showed that following installation it can take several years before the formaldehyde level falls to normal. However, it's worth noting that the number of people affected is very small indeed.

Sloppy installation of cavity insulation can lead to the damp course's being bridged, and it is vital to employ a firm that surveys the property first and will guarantee their work. Choose one registered with the British Standards Institute and approved by the

Agrement Board. In new houses cavity-wall insulation in sheet form may be installed during construction but this will not fill the cavity.

Solid walls can be insulated from the inside or the outside. Inside the house walls can be lined with **thermal plasterboard**, which is ordinary plasterboard with a layer of expanded polystyrene fixed to the back. It comes in a range of thicknesses from 15 mm (½ in) to 60 mm (2⅜ in). The boards are stuck to the old wall with adhesive and held in place with screws and wallplugs while it sets, and they can then be plastered or finished by ordinary dry lining methods. The one hitch with this technique is that plumbing, wiring and skirting boards will all have to be re-sited.

Simpler is using a **wall lining**, which comes on a roll like wallpaper and is fixed in the same way. One make consists of a 5-mm sandwich of foam rubber and glass-fibre fleece. It can be decorated over and is particularly good for combating condensation on a cold wall.

A specialist firm will have to be called in to insulate the outside walls and the expense is such that it is probably worth doing only where the wall is in poor condition and needs rendering anyway. The method used may be applying a render containing an insulating material like polystyrene or fixing slabs of insulation to the wall and rendering over it. Make sure the contractor uses an Agrement-approved system and belongs to the External Wall Insulation Association.

Lofts: In the mid-sixties when the Building Regulations were being devised 25 mm (1 in) of insulation between the joists was specified. Today 100 mm (4 in) is regarded as the minimum thickness and 150 mm (6 in) is preferable. However, if the insulation protrudes higher than the tops of the joists it makes it difficult to use the loft for storage. You are also likely to plunge through the ceiling occasionally because you can't see where you are walking. A **mineral-wool** or **glass-fibre** blanket should be laid between the joists. If it's too wide, trim it with a saw while it is still in the roll. Where the joists have irregular spaces between them, **loose-fill mineral wool** or **vermiculite chips** can be spread about.

If ventilation under the eaves is going to be restricted, holes should be cut in the soffit or air-bricks inserted in the gable end. Insulation should not be laid under the cold-water storage tank as it is often only the heat rising from the house that prevents it from freezing in the winter. Instead, wrap the tank in a mineral-wool blanket or box it in with 50-mm (2-in) expanded polystyrene board or buy a custom-made tank-jacket. Cover all exposed water pipes with 15-mm (⅝-in) foam sleeves and use a flexible mastic to block the holes where they enter the ceiling, usually in or near the airing cupboard. Stick a piece of polystyrene board to the back of the loft hatch and put draught-excluders round the edge.

Cylinders: The hot-water cylinder must be insulated. Nowadays insulation is applied at the factory but an 80-mm (3⅛-in) insulating jacket can be bought to clothe a naked cylinder. The saving is estimated to be up to £50 a year.

Radiators: These should have a reflecting panel stuck behind them which throws heat back into the room and prevents it from being absorbed by the wall. It's a cheap improvement and will soon pay for itself, particularly where the walls are poorly insulated.

Floors: A solid floor should be insulated during construction by polystyrene or rigid foam slabs which are laid under the damp-proof membrane before the final screed goes down. The usual problem with suspended floors, particularly if they are stained and varnished, is gale-force draughts between the boards. Block them up by using masking tape underneath or by filling them with papier mâché or, much quicker but much more expensive, with a gun-operated sealant.

One way of tackling the problem is to create a new floor by laying hardboard over sheet insulation or by using flooring-grade chipboard to which a layer of insulation has been attached. Loose-fill insulation can be inserted under the floor and held in plastic netting stapled across the joists. It is important not to fill the cavity completely or ventilation will be prevented.

Windows and doors: Double glazing is often thought to be the answer to heat loss, but only about 10 per cent of the escaping warmth gets out through the windows and the saving resulting from installing two layers of glass is never going to match the expense. Double glazing is worth considering only where windows are going to have to be replaced anyway. Sealed double-glazing units can have gaps between the panes of 6 mm (¼-in), 12 mm (½ in) or 20 mm (¾ in). The larger the gap the more effective the insulation. Efficiency is further improved if one of the panes is **Low-E glass**. Low-E stands for low emissivity and it means the surface of the glass is slightly coated to reflect heat back into the room. Sealed units may have air trapped between the two layers of glass or an inert gas such as argon may be used. If condensation appears in the gap it means the seal has been breached in some way.

Secondary glazing is cheaper and uses a second pane of glass fitted against the window frame inside the house. Even cheaper is a sheet of plastic film applied to the window with double-sided tape and a hair-drier. Another type of window film is slightly tinted and contains metal particles which reflect heat back into the room in the same way as Low-E glass. A recent innovation is a form of **triple glazing** using two layers of transparent film held in a PVC frame which is fitted to the existing window frame.

Thermal shutters and **roller blinds** are widely used abroad to keep the heat in at night when the house is usually at its warmest and the outside temperature is at its lowest. The design of British windows has restricted their use here, but a number of systems is now available. They have the added advantage of making the house more impregnable to burglars.

Despite all the technology that's available, don't forget one of the most effective, cheapest and simplest answers to the problem of stopping heat escaping through the windows — a set of thick and well-lined curtains.

Designing the perfect draught-excluder seems to be one of the obsessions of every self-respecting inventor, and the variety of solutions to the problem of cold wind whistling up the trouser leg or skirt is quite wonderful to behold. Self-adhesive strips of foam that fit round doors and windows are cheap and easy but tend not to last long. There are also self-adhesive brush strips and tubes of plastic that can be squeezed between door or window and frame, but these, too, tend to come off before too long. More effective, but more expensive, are brush or wiper seals in plastic or aluminium that are nailed on. **Silicone sealant** ensures a good tight fit on windows. A line of silicone is piped round, the window closed and not opened until the silicone has cured, and the result is a layer on the frame that perfectly matches the irregularities of the window.

9

DAMP, ROT AND PESTS

'All human things are subject to decay,
And, when fate summons, monarchs must obey.'
(John Dryden [1631-1700]: Mac Flecknoe*)*

In Genesis, the Greatest DIY Expert of All recommends Noah to daub his Ark 'within and without in pitch', demonstrating that the Almighty was keenly aware of the perils awaiting untreated timber. Damp-loving fungi and animal and insect pests have been responsible for the destruction of far more buildings than wars, fires and natural disasters, and the forces of decay have not been turned back one bit by the march of science. In medieval times wood was often charred or pickled in brine in an attempt to preserve the structure of a house. Today we rely on complex chemicals and sensible guttering to do the job. But many homes still resound in the quiet of the night to the drip of water and the chomping jaws of the ravenous larvae of *anobium punctatum* (better known as woodworm).

Finding a reliable contractor to carry out damp-proofing and rot and pest control work is essential. It is estimated that about 600 firms come and go every year, making it difficult to be certain about the value of a guarantee. Conditions of contracts also vary a good deal. Some rot-proofing companies won't give an estimate without doing exploratory work and this could cost hundreds of pounds in itself. Look for members of bodies like the British Chemical Dampcourse Association and British Wood Preserving Association who have a code of practice. Go through the same routine as for finding a builder: check out their reputation, ask for the names of recent customers to contact, and so on.

DAMP

Apart from causing an unpleasant smell and the inconvenience of wallpaper peeling faster than the British in Benidorm, persistent damp will lead to fungal infestations and structural failure. The number of homes seriously affected by damp in Britain is estimated at two million, and the number with some damp problem is many times more than that. There are four fundamental causes of damp:

★ **Penetration:** The causes are usually simple to deal with once they are identified. Loose or missing tiles, blocked gutters or downspout hoppers and broken rainwater pipes are only too obvious. Other causes can be much more elusive, however.

When an apparently sound roof lets in water many fruitless hours can be spent in the loft with a torch following the meandering path of drips along rafters and purlins in an attempt to discover where they originated. The problem is that where the water first appears may be a long way from where it entered the roof, and it is likely to have made its way secretively along the top of a rafter before leaping out at you. Flashing on valleys and around chimneys can crack with age and a hairline fracture can be almost impossible to spot. Decades of water dripping off a slate on to lead can wear a hole not much bigger than a pinprick, and when it starts to rain it is amazing what volume of water will make its way through. Back pointing of slates from inside the roof space can also cause problems by creating little dams which collect rain-water. With painstaking detective work, though, the source of the water should be narrowed down to an area where close inspection will discover the leak. If it doesn't, the only answer is a general overhaul of the area and crossed fingers.

All modern roofs are **underfelted** to catch drips should a tile come loose and to prevent rain and snow from being blown in through the spaces between the tiles or slates. An old roof that consistently lets in water should be underfelted but it's an expensive job as all the slates and tiles will have to come off first. A cheaper, recent alternative is having a weatherproof layer of polyurethane foam sprayed on to the underside of the roof by a contractor. This has the advantage of providing insulation and holding the tiles in place, and because it is unseen it doesn't detract from the appearance of the roof like external coatings that can be applied.

In older houses where there is no cavity between the walls water can make its way straight through them. Repointing may be all that is required, but older bricks are sometimes very porous and may need to be treated with a **waterproofing spray**. Alternatively, the wall could be rendered with cement or painted with a cement- or stone-based paint.

Window and door frames may shrink away from the walls and let in water. Seal the cracks with a flexible mastic. Well-made windows should have a **drip-groove** underneath to prevent water from creeping from the edge of the sill back to the wall. Check that this hasn't been clogged with paint. If the groove is absent a piece of square 6-mm (¼-in) beading should be pinned on to give the same effect.

⋆ **Rising:** The absence of a damp-proof course (DPC) will naturally invite moisture into the house. Where there is one it may have become ineffective with age or **bridged** by a flower bed or by a heap of coal piled against the wall above the level of the DPC. Excess mortar dropped in the wall cavity can have the same effect, as can wall ties covered with mortar as a result of sloppy workmanship.

Where a damp-proof course is absent or erratic a new one will have to be installed. The most effective is a **physical** barrier to damp in the form of a polythene, lead or bituminous layer. It can be inserted by the removal of a number of bricks a section at a time or the mortar course can be cut with a special saw.

A **chemical** DPC uses silicone which impregnates the brick or stonework to form an invisible barrier against water. The contractor will drill holes in the brick 150 mm (6 in) above ground level and insert silicone under pressure. The other method is to drill the mortar and let the silicone flow in under the force of gravity. Inside the house the damaged plaster must be removed and replaced with a sand and cement render that has a waterproofing agent added. This is to prevent damp already in the wall from emerging and staining a new topcoat of plaster with the salts it carries.

Electro-osmosis damp-proofing relies on an electrical charge run through rods inserted in the wall to prevent moisture from rising. There is doubt about the effectiveness of this, as there is about the **ceramic tube** method, whereby hollow tubes are inserted in the wall and the water is said to evaporate through them.

A solid floor will be damp if no damp-proof membrane has been laid in it or if the membrane was damaged during construction. Try painting the floor with a bituminous sealing agent or, even better, a liquid rubber waterproofer, but beware that sealing the floor doesn't then send the damp creeping up the walls. This is a common problem in basements and cellars, and the answer is to **tank** the room or seal the floor and walls against damp. One way is to batten the walls and cover them with plasterboard with a plastic vapour barrier sandwiched between. Another method is to use a corrugated waterproof lathing which is attached to the wall and plastered over. Recently 'paint-on' moisture barriers have been developed. The old plaster is knocked off and the wall made good. One technique requires the wall to be rendered with a sand and cement mix with a waterproofer added before the moisture barrier is applied. Another product is applied to the wall and the waterproof render applied over it. The damp-proof membrane in the floor is bonded to the moisture barrier on the wall before plastering, thus sealing the room against moisture.

Where the amount of damp in a wall is slight you can line it by sticking a pitch-coated paper, aluminium foil or foil-backed plasterboard to it, or by painting it with a waterproofing liquid. There's a wide range of remedies around and it's a good idea to seek advice from your friendly neighbourhood builders' merchant.

⋆ **Leaks:** Those decorative but unwelcome stains on the ceiling may be caused by leaking plumbing or an overflowing water-storage tank in the loft. Check that the valve and overflow from the cistern are working properly, and suspect a leaky pipe if the pipes are unlagged and there has been a recent freeze.

⋆ **Condensation:** This is one of the biggest causes of rot and it is largely a modern problem. When houses were so draughty that aeroplane designs could have been tested in the hall, condensation was kept at bay. Today, however, ventilation is much reduced by a high degree of insulation, heating and draughtproofing. Meanwhile there are appliances such as showers, washing machines and tumble driers that pour moisture into the air.

The warmer the air gets the more it acts like a sponge soaking up water vapour. But it can hold only a limited amount of moisture and when that limit is reached the air is said to have a **relative humidity (rh)** of 100 per cent. Breathe out once this level has been reached and the moisture will find a surface to start condensing on. But the real trouble comes when warm, moisture-laden air comes into contact with a cold surface such as a window pane or an uninsulated outside wall. As it cools it can't carry its load of moisture and it promptly jettisons it in droplets that soon assemble into a stream. Two people cooking, washing and breathing will pump out four litres of water a day. A family of five produces seven litres. Run the tumble drier, have a bath and do the ironing and the water will be practically lapping round your feet.

The obvious answer to the problem of condensation is better ventilation which will provide a change of air that can keep mopping it up. Where condensation is visible the simplest remedy is to open the window, but this can lead to complaints of frost-bite from people using the bathroom in the depths of winter. An extractor fan fitted in the wall or window will get rid of the moisture-laden air and combat condensation by throwing the soggy air outside. However, it will also throw out the air you have spent money heating.

An alternative is to buy a **dehumidifier**. This works a bit like a fridge, having an evaporator coil which cools the air and allows the resulting water to drip down into a container that can be emptied when full. The dry air is then warmed before being returned to the room. Dehumidifiers are cheap to run and you can use the condensed water they produce to top up batteries and steam irons. But some people find the noise of the fan irritating, and they are much less efficient at low temperatures because the air contains much less water. Cheap 'miracle' cures offered in the newspaper small ads are usually water-absorbing crystals or special paints. The amount of the water the crystals can absorb is obviously very limited before they have to be dried out. This can be done in the oven, but that merely sends the water vapour back into the house where it came from. The paints help to control condensation by acting as a sponge and absorbing water, but again the capacity is very limited. However, a fungicide in the paint will control the mould that results from condensation.

Streaming walls and windows are a nuisance but condensation in concealed places such as the roof can even cause structural damage. As well as the natural moisture content of timber (up to 20 per cent), and vapour from an uncovered water cistern, water vapour from the house can also penetrate the thin plasterboard used for ceilings. Before the war a draughty roof space was in no peril, but the use of felt has restricted the escape route for moisture. As a result, mould and fungal growth thrives and crucial pieces of metal such as nail plates may corrode. To combat this, a recent development has been **roofing felt** which contains tiny holes that won't let water droplets in but will let vapour out. However, this is the answer only in a new home or in one being reroofed.

Water vapour can be prevented from rising into the roof space by a sheet of polythene incorporated into the ceiling, but this is really practicable only during the construction process. It can also cause condensation problems in the bedrooms because the vapour can't escape upwards. Much better is to ensure that the roof space is properly ventilated, and the usual way to do this is with a vent in the soffits.

Houses with a roof pitch of 15° or more need openings equivalent to a 10-mm (3⁄8-in) gap along the soffit on either side of the house. If the pitch is less than 15° a 25-mm (1-in) gap is necessary. The holes are covered with a patent grid or wire mesh to keep out birds.

GUIDE TO DAMP PROBLEMS

A. Faulty flashing.
B. Missing tiles.
C. Ivy on wall.
D. Gutters blocked by leaves.
E. Overflow from cistern.
F. Peeling paint on cladding allows water entry.
G. Cracked down-pipe.
H. Leak from toilet.
I. Defective pointing between bricks.
J. Condensation on windows.
K. Dirty wall tie bridging cavity.
L. Leak from bath outlet.
M. Leak from down-pipe joint.
N. Blocked hopper.
O. Cracked paint on window frames.
P. Blocked air-brick.
Q. Ineffective groove under sill.
R. Impervious floor covering allows moisture to build up.
S. Blocked air-hole in sleeper wall.
T. Blocked drain.
U. Wall-plate in contact with adjacent wall surface.
V. Soil heaped above damp-proof course.
W. Foundations damaged by tree roots.
X. Flood water on oversite.
Y. No damp-proof membrane.
Z. No damp-proof course under wall-plate.

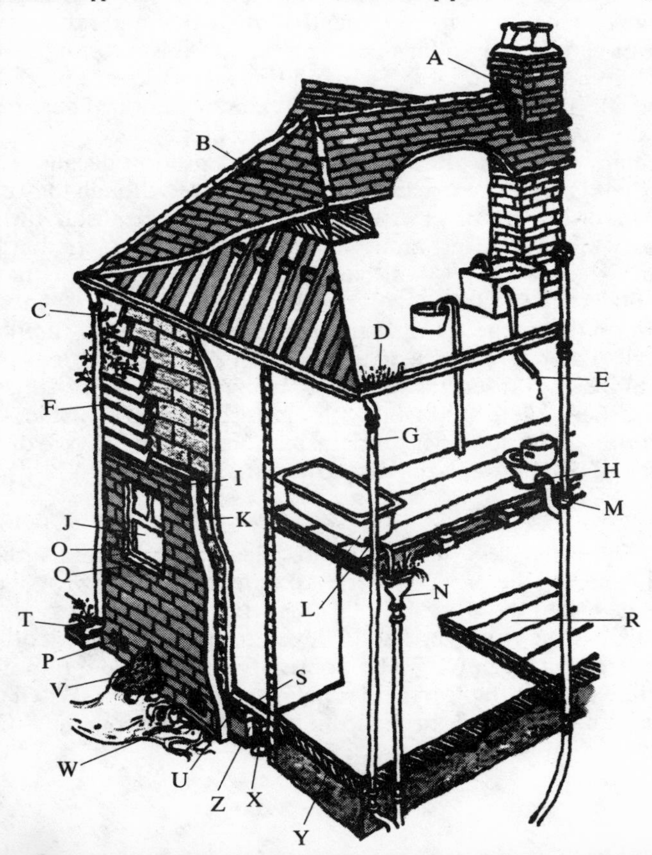

Where insulation restricts the flow of air from the vent, an **eaves vent** which is a kind of tube is needed to provide a path through the insulation. In complex roofs where air pockets can remain undisturbed in corners, **ridge vents** or **tile vents** may need to be installed. Air-bricks for use in a gable end are available but these are not acceptable for new work or for major alterations.

Flat roofs used to be very vulnerable to condensation and it wasn't uncommon to see fibreboard and chipboard swelling, distorting and even breaking up after only a few years. The reason is that insulation was placed immediately over the ceiling, which left a cold enclosed space between the insulation and the roof membrane. Nowadays these **cold deck** roofs have to have a 25-mm (10-in) opening to provide ventilation, but the better solution is a **warm deck** roof. These have the insulation immediately below the roof membrane so that the gap underneath is at room temperature.

Lack of ventilation under floors can lead to joists rotting gently away while nobody notices. To avoid this air-bricks are placed in both outside and sleeper walls to permit air circulation. These must not be allowed to become blocked or covered up.

Basement walls are often subject to condensation because they are kept cold by the damp earth behind them even though they may be dry themselves. An electric heater with a thermostat turned down very low can be left on at the base of the wall to combat the problem — some models will hardly use any more power than a light bulb. Other solutions are to line the wall with sheets of expanded polystyrene or, in extreme cases, to build a complete inner wall. This could just be plasterboard fixed to wall battens with a layer of insulation such as rock wool behind. Even more efficient would be a complete stud wall with plasterboard on both sides of the partition and a double layer of insulation, one on the face of the old wall and one between the plasterboard.

ROT

A surveyor investigating a house for his clients found several indications of damp on the ground floor. 'Are you aware of any rot in the house?' he asked the owner. Without a word this man crossed the room to what the surveyor had believed to be a long, low coffee-table covered with a cloth. With a flourish the householder removed the cloth, exposing the top two feet of an upright piano. When the instrument had plunged through the badly rotten floor, the house owner's phlegmatic solution had been to convert it into an item of furniture. Admirable though this response may have been, more direct action is recommended to deal with the problem of rot.

Wet rot is the general name for several fungi which attack timber that is constantly damp. It is the commonest type of rot and the symptoms are the discoloration of timber until it is dark brown or black and wood becoming spongy when wet and brittle when dry. You can treat it by cutting away the affected timber and treating the remainder with a fungicide.

Neglected window frames are commonly ravaged by wet rot, some of them so badly that the frame rots through completely and the tenons of the joints are exposed. Confronted with this horrible sight many home-owners will give up and order new frames. But quite severely damaged windows can be repaired. The affected softened wood should be scraped or cut out and all the exposed wood treated with a preservative fluid. In order to prevent further attacks by the fungi the good parts of the frame should be drilled and pellets inserted which will combat any further infestation. Then a resin-based wood-repair compound should be used to fill the holes. Working with a small trowel try to get it as near as possible to the original shape and then sand it flush when it has hardened. The frame can now be primed ready for painting.

Modern roof timbers and joists are pressure-treated with preservative. Old ones are not and, as a result, are vulnerable to wet rot. A leaky roof can encourage an outbreak but timbers are also at risk where they meet walls. The coldness of the brick or stonework can attract condensation, or the walls may be full of rising damp. Depending on the extent of the damage a surveyor or building inspector should be called in to assess the situation. Whether a joist has a new section bolted on or is completely replaced, the wood should first be treated with a water-repellent timber preservative such as Cuprinol and the ends wrapped in a damp-proof membrane or painted with a bitumen preparation before it is inserted back in the wall.

Dry rot is much nastier than wet rot and much harder to deal with, and may require extensive destruction of timber, brickwork and mortar to make sure every trace has been eradicated. As a result many people may prefer to call in a specialist firm to tackle the fungus that has rightly been called 'the cancer of wood'.

The first sign of dry rot may be a dank, mushroomy smell. Look for small whitish rubbery growths like malignant truffles along the edge of skirting boards or between the joints in panelling. These will expand and open up, allowing vast numbers of reddish-brown airborne spores to fill the house. If the first indication of the fungus is brown dust blowing up through cracks in floorboards or settling on cupboard shelves it means that significant damage has already been done. Cottony strands from the fungus can penetrate masonry and the earth under floors to reach fresh timber and start a new colony. They can quickly spread from cellar to attic, or from next door into your house.

To reveal the extent of the damage anything that might be hiding it must be stripped away, including plaster and brickwork. Some experts recommend that no matter how small the fungus, an area of 3 sq m (32 sq ft) must be opened up around it, and that when the last trace has been discovered you go another metre (three feet) beyond that point. It is at this point that the despairing householder begins to think it may be easier to knock the house down and start again. All affected timber must be burned, and sound wood up to a metre beyond the infection must also go on the bonfire. The remaining timber and brickwork must be treated with a fungicide. Don't forget that the house is still full of spores just itching to germinate and start a fresh outbreak, so it is essential to remove the cause of damp that allowed the fungus to get started and ventilation must be ensured in every cupboard and cavity.

PESTS

Woodworm: The commonest threat to timber is *anobium punctatum*, the furniture beetle. Its common name may suggest that it is something of a gourmet among insects, relishing only chairs and tables, but all unpainted and untreated structural timbers can suffer an attack of the anobiums. The beetle flies into a house and finds a crack in a suitable piece of timber in which to lay its eggs. When the larvae, known as woodworms, hatch they start tunnelling their way through the wood until after about three years it is a mass of galleries and so weakened that the merest tap can result in a much-loved piece of Sheraton or equally appreciated section of purlin collapsing in a cloud of dust. There is no obvious sign of woodworms until they abandon their home as fully fledged beetles, leaving small exit holes behind them. Through these holes will pour the fine dust that is evidence of a woodworm attack. The treatment is to brush or spray affected timber with a proprietary brand of woodworm-killer and to inject the chemical into the holes through the tapered nozzle that usually comes with the product. This is to make sure that any grubs still remaining in the timber are killed. Goggles and a mask should always be worn when you are spraying and it may be wiser to leave the job to a contractor if the infestation is a serious one. Upholstered items can be treated by fumigation by a specialist firm.

Death-watch beetles: These are unlikely to be found in modern houses unless timbers from old ones have been used in their construction. As in the case of the furniture beetle the damage is done by boring grubs and they prefer damp timber already softened by fungal infection. Treat by spraying and injecting an insecticide and remove the cause of damp that attracted the insect in the first place. The beetle is believed to have acquired the 'watch' part of its name because of the characteristic ticking noise both sexes make before mating. It has been suggested that this was often heard by those sitting with the sick or dying at night, which would explain the reference to death. However, it is possible that people were aware that the noise may quickly be followed by an unexpected trip to the afterlife following a sudden roof collapse.

House longhorn beetles: These are the largest wood-borers leaving ½ inch oval holes in the sapwood of softwood timbers, but are found only in certain areas of the south of England. They should be dealt with in the same way as woodworm.

Cockroaches: These are mercifully rare in houses but are very difficult to get rid of. They are one of the most successful insects, having been around almost unchanged for 250 million years, and the haphazard squirting of an insecticide powder is not going to impress them. A variety of attacks, persistence and expert advice is essential.

Mice and rats: Field mice may abandon a chilly field for the warmth of a house in autumn or winter, while house mice are determined to become permanent guests. Apart from the damage they do chewing pipes and wiring and spoiling food, they seem to spend all night charging up and down wall and ceiling cavities wearing heavy boots, an activity that makes sleep impossible. Many mice are now immune to Warfarin-type baits, so they should be caught with the traditional spring traps or killed with a humane poison such as Alphakil, or by being shown videos of Paul Daniels. Modern poisons are far less dangerous than common household items like bleach or metal polish, but to ensure peace of mind bait can be laid in specially designed boxes where it is safe from pets and children.

Rats are unlikely to invade a house but they can infest outbuildings and outside food stores. Waterproof bait should be laid for outdoor use. Because rats can carry serious diseases the local authority must be informed of any infestation.

Houses may be invaded by a whole range of annoying but less destructive insects, from ants and cat fleas to carpet beetles, silverfish and fire brats. There is a variety of sprays and powders available to control these. If you're in doubt, the local authority pest-control unit will be able to give advice.

10

BUILDING TECHNIQUES

'Build it up with bricks and mortar,
Bricks and mortar, bricks and mortar,
Build it up with bricks and mortar,
My fair lady.'
(Nursery rhyme: London Bridge Is Falling Down)

Ambitious do-it-yourselfers may wish at some stage to alter the fabric of their property or extend it. This chapter outlines what's involved in surrounding folk with four walls and a roof. For those who have no intention in developing a close relationship with cement and scaffolding, the following is intended to help them talk the same language as builders and to understand their tribal customs.

TOOLS OF THE TRADE

The rule with tools is to go for the best you can afford. A good shovel and a wheelbarrow are the first things anyone contemplating heavier work needs to think about. But barrows designed to shift leaves from the lawn will probably give up the ghost after a couple of loads of concrete. The professional will also choose a steel-shafted shovel with a sturdy blade.

Other tools for general building work would include a **trowel**, which is used for applying mortar to bricks. A small one is easier to use for repairing pointing. A steel **float** is used to give concrete and plaster a smooth finish, while a wooden float provides a rougher finish. A **hawk** is a plastic or wooden tray with a handle, which looks rather like a bird table, and carries mortar or plaster to the float, or throws it on the floor when your attention wanders.

A long **spirit level** with bubbles for checking vertical and horizontal work, a **string line** with two pins, a **plumb-line**, a **club hammer** and a **bolster chisel** are needed for brickwork. Gloves or a barrier cream can be used as protection against cement which can cause nasty cracks in soft hands. For big jobs that require a cement-mixer you can hire a small cement-mixer from the local tool-hire emporium.

Remember that ladders may be fine for cleaning the windows, but are not ideal things to work off, particularly if you need both hands free or are shifting weights about. Hire a scaffolding tower or independent scaffolding rather than risk a fall.

MATERIALS

Cement: This is the glue that holds your home together, unless you happen to live in one of those mud huts we were discussing earlier. Like plaster it doesn't keep and if you're going to brave using it, buy it as fresh as possible. Cement does not work by water evaporation. Instead, mixing with water allows a chemical reaction to take place, and in hot weather already activated cement must be kept damp by being covered with plastic or sprayed to keep the reaction going. Wet cement must not be allowed to freeze and a frost-proofing agent can be added to the water in chilly weather. A sulphate-resistant cement will be needed where it will be in contact with certain clay or peat soils.

Mortar: When cement is mixed with sand it makes the mortar that is sandwiched between bricks and stone. There are a number of different mortar mixes, but 1 part cement to 4 parts soft sand works for most things. Novices sometimes panic that a mix may not be strong enough and add far too much cement. Not only is this wasteful but it makes the mortar liable to shrinkage, and this can crack the joints or even the bricks. Lime can be added to mortar to make it buttery and easy to work, but now a plasticizer such as Febmix is more often used to get the same effect. A squirt of washing-up liquid will do at a pinch.

Concrete: Apart from providing Mafia victims with an unconventional wardrobe, concrete has revolutionized the building industry. This versatile mixture contains cement, sand and an **aggregate** such as gravel, and it is the aggregate that gives concrete its strength. The sharp angular particles of an aggregate like crushed green granite lock together to produce an extremely durable concrete. Uncrushed river gravel is rounder and less strong but easier to work with.

A mix for heavy-duty work like the construction of foundations and floor slabs would be 1 part cement to 2½ parts sand and 4 parts coarse aggregate. For paths and thin section work try 1 part cement to 2 parts sand and 3 parts aggregate. For a smooth finishing surface or **screed** to a concrete floor use 1 part cement to 4 parts sand and no aggregate.

Ready-mixed concrete to which you need only add water can be bought from DIY stores and is suitable for small jobs. For bigger jobs it is worthwhile buying the ingredients separately and hiring a mixer. However the ingredients are combined it is essential that the sand, aggregate and cement be measured out beforehand and mixed thoroughly before water is added.

For work requiring more than 3 cubic metres it's probably easier and no dearer to have ready-mixed concrete delivered by lorry. If you do decide to buy concrete this way make sure the site is completely ready to receive it as it sets fast and you may end up with an unwanted concrete sculpture in the middle of your premises. If the concrete will need to be moved by barrow to the job it is advisable to have pressganged or bribed some helpers beforehand, as it should be laid within about two hours of delivery — and since a cubic metre of cement weighs nearly 1½ tons this is no small job. When concrete has to fill a particular shape it must be **shuttered** with pieces of timber that will take the weight. Err on the side of safety when it comes to reinforcing. One builder we know who was working in a basement to underpin the house's foundations found himself up to his neck in concrete when the shuttering collapsed.

LAYING CONCRETE DRIVES AND PATHS

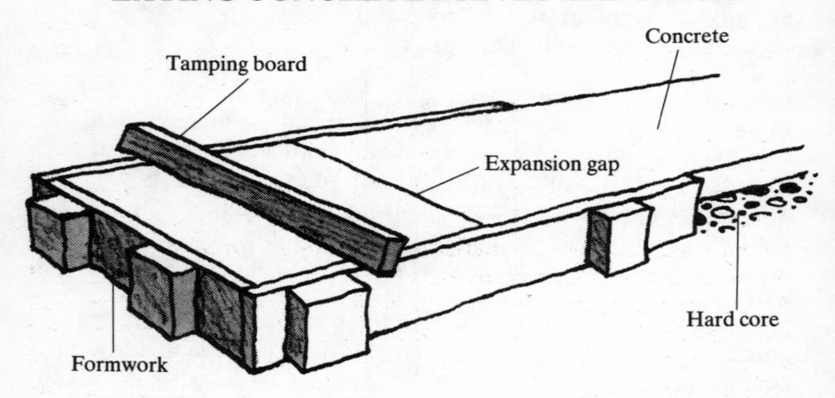

Concrete can stand a great deal of pressure in the form of **compression**, as it does under the weight of a house. But it is not strong under **tension**, for example when bearing the weight of a wall while spanning a large window. This is why concrete lintels usually have reinforcing bars built into them. Reinforcing wire mesh is also used in concrete foundations to protect them against any earth movement.

Concrete paths and drives should be laid not less than 100 mm (4 in) thick on top of well-compacted hard core, which is another word for rubble. Wooden formwork will be needed — boards pegged on the outside to take the weight of the concrete and to provide a guide to the height. A wooden **tamping** board can be worked across the shuttering to give an even finish to the concrete. The surface should be left slightly rough and not trowelled smooth to prevent skidding and slipping in wet weather. A concrete drive can be laid simply as two strips for the wheels, but a full-width one should be laid in 3-m (10-ft) sections with boards between them. When they are removed the gaps can be filled with sand or cold asphalt to allow the slabs to expand in hot weather without cracking.

Always cover fresh concrete with polythene sheeting or some other suitable material if it is in danger of drying out too quickly and crazing and dusting up. Curing will take four days in warm weather and up to ten in the winter, and it will be getting on for a month before maximum strength is reached.

Bricks: Kentish stocks, Accrington reds, Staffordshire blues, gaults, wirecuts and Flettons — there is a gritty romance about the names of bricks that bring to mind the nomenclature of moths or fishermen's flies. Each type is distinguished by the geology and the manufacturing process of its locality.

Despite the variety of bricks they all fall into three basic categories. **Facing** bricks are used for the external structure of a house and combine good looks with good weathering qualities. The colour range includes all shades of red through yellow and brown to purple and black. **Commons** are cheaper than facings and are used for construction that will not be visible, for example in internal walls that will be plastered. **Engineering** bricks are very dense and waterproof and are used wherever great strength is needed, i.e. for chimney tops and copings, and underground structures such as manholes.

A standard brick measures 215 mm by 102.5 mm by 65 mm (roughly 8½ in by 4 in by 2⅝ in), although non-standard bricks are also made for special jobs. To calculate the number of bricks needed for a job a 10-mm (⅜-in) width of mortar has to be taken into consideration and this gives a nominal size of 225 mm by 112.5 mm by 75 mm (8⅞ in by 4⅜ in by 3 in). The size of a brick building should be a multiple of the nominal size in order to avoid cutting a lot of bricks in half, one of the less interesting ways to pass the time. When it has to be done, cut a groove with a bolster chisel and hit the unwanted bit hard. Professionals do it perfectly every time with the curved side of a trowel but amateurs end up with an assortment of oddly-shaped half-bricks. However, practice makes perfect.

Blocks: These are used for building the inner leaf of a cavity wall. They are made in larger sizes than bricks, the nominal dimensions usually being 450 mm by 225 mm (roughly 17¾ in by 8⅞ in). But they are designed to **course up** with bricks to allow ties to be inserted horizontally between them. The thickness of blocks ranges from 50 mm (2 in) upwards but 100 mm (4 in) and 150 mm (6 in) are the common sizes. Blocks are made from clay, concrete or a lightweight aggregate such as clinker. Dense concrete blocks are used below the damp-course level. Above the DPC, clinker blocks like breeze blocks have generally been replaced by aerated concrete blocks such as Celcon and Thermalite which are easy to cut with a saw and have good insulation properties. The insulation properties of a building material are defined as its **U-value**. The use of a 150-mm thick thermal block will satisfy the current Building Regulations on U-values and avoid the need for some form of cavity insulation. Building blocks can be load-bearing or non-loadbearing, depending on the job the wall must do.

Plaster: This is made from a mineral called gypsum, and building plaster is a close relation of the stuff that gets wrapped round broken legs. Like cement, plaster must be fresh and it is no good holding on to a half-empty bag for six months and expecting it to be usable. After it is opened keep it in a tightly sealed plastic bag to help prolong its life.

Traditionally plaster is applied in two stages: for the undercoat a **browning** is used and this is covered with a **finishing** coat. There are different finishing plasters and it is important that the one chosen is compatible with the undercoat. Recently one-coat plasters have been introduced to make life easier for do-it-yourselfers and this dries to a white finish rather than the usual pinky-brown.

FOUNDATIONS

An average two-storey home weighs about 100 tons, so its downward pressure is massive. To cope with this the building needs a firm foundation, and the type and depth depends on the size of the building and the nature of the subsoil.

Most houses are built on **strip** foundations. Given reasonable subsoil, a trench 1 metre (3 ft 3 in) deep is dug and concrete poured in the bottom. The strip will usually be about 300-450 mm (12-18 in) deep and twice the width of the wall it will support. Strip foundations must be deep enough to remain untroubled by shrinkage of the earth in drought conditions or by the effects of extreme cold or heavy rain. Compact gravel or sandy gravel is well drained and provides good foundations, but clay is a problem for the builder as it expands and contracts during wet and dry spells, and this expansion produces an unpleasant condition called **clayheave** which can move foundations. The answer is to leave a gap or 'expansion space' or to insert a special type of panel which collapses when wet and leaves the desired elbow room for the clay.

All topsoil must be cleared from the site before work on the foundations can begin. After the trench is dug wooden pegs will be inserted in the bottom as a guide to the depth of concrete required. The concrete is poured in to the height of the peg, and the building inspector will first make sure that the correct height of peg is showing indicating that the foundations are the proper depth. But it is not unknown for cowboy builders to wait until the inspector has gone home and then knock all the pegs down a few inches before the concrete goes in — thus saving themselves a lot of money on concrete and possibly imperilling the building into the bargain.

A **raft** foundation is like a large concrete slab and may be used where the subsoil is uneven in density and settlement could result. It is also used for small buildings that are to have solid floors, such as garages and garden sheds. Round the perimeter of the raft a small trench should be dug to permit a concrete **rib** to be created. This will prevent the hard core from being squeezed out and water from getting under.

Pile foundations are used for extremely large buildings and where the subsoil is very poor. These are essentially tubes of concrete sunk deep into the ground to support strips.

WALLS

Every two-year-old construction worker piling up wooden blocks learns pretty quickly that the edifice is likely to stay together better if the joints between the bricks on one course come in the middle of the bricks on the course below. This is known as the **stretcher bond** method and is the way full-size builders also put the bricks together when the wall is a single brick thick. Garages, garden buildings and support walls for conservatories and so on will usually be stretcher bond brickwork. Note that the Building Regulations don't allow these walls to be more than 3 m (10 ft) high and they should have support **piers** — columns usually created with a double thickness of brick — at the ends and in the middle if needed.

BRICK BONDS (STRETCHER, ENGLISH, FLEMISH)

Stretcher bond

English bond

Flemish bond

Some walls are made two bricks thick and are tied together with **headers**, bricks placed across the wall so that the short end (the header) is showing. **English bond** alternates a course of stretchers with a course of headers. **Flemish bond** has alternate headers and stretchers in the same course.

Brickwork starts with the ends or corners of the walls being built up. A horizontal bed of mortar is laid and the end of the brick 'buttered' with mortar and laid in place with the **frog** or recessed side upwards. The courses are kept straight by the use of a string set straight with a spirit level. To make sure the courses are rising evenly a **gauge rod** should be used. This is a piece of timber with marks every 75 mm (3 in) — the height of the brick plus a 10-mm (3/8-in) allowance for the mortar. If there is an internal wall then this should be raised at the same time as there is a risk that a strong wind will blow a high, single-brick wall over. The usual width of the cavity is 50 mm (2 in).

Cavity walls are held together with **ties** inserted in the mortar of the joints no more than 900 mm (36 in) apart horizontally and 450 mm (18 in) vertically. Ties are usually made from galvanized sheet metal or wire, but these may push the wall out of line if they rust, and to avoid this risk ties are now made in polypropylene. Mortar mustn't drop on to ties or the damp-proof course might be bridged. After ties have been inserted a batten the width of the cavity should be placed on them to catch any dropped mortar as the work continues.

The damp-proof course is what stops the moisture in the earth being drawn up the bricks into the wall. It is just polythene or bituminous felt rolled out on to a bed of mortar and covered with another bed before the next course of bricks goes on. It should be inserted 150 mm (6 in) above soil level. Although DPCs are specified under the Building Regulations for inhabited buildings it is a good idea and no trouble to insert them also in garages and workshops.

A DPC is required wherever the cavity wall is closed off to take a window or door. It should run between the frame and the wall and then be inserted vertically between the bricks that are closing the cavity.

STEEL BOX AND CONCRETE LINTELS

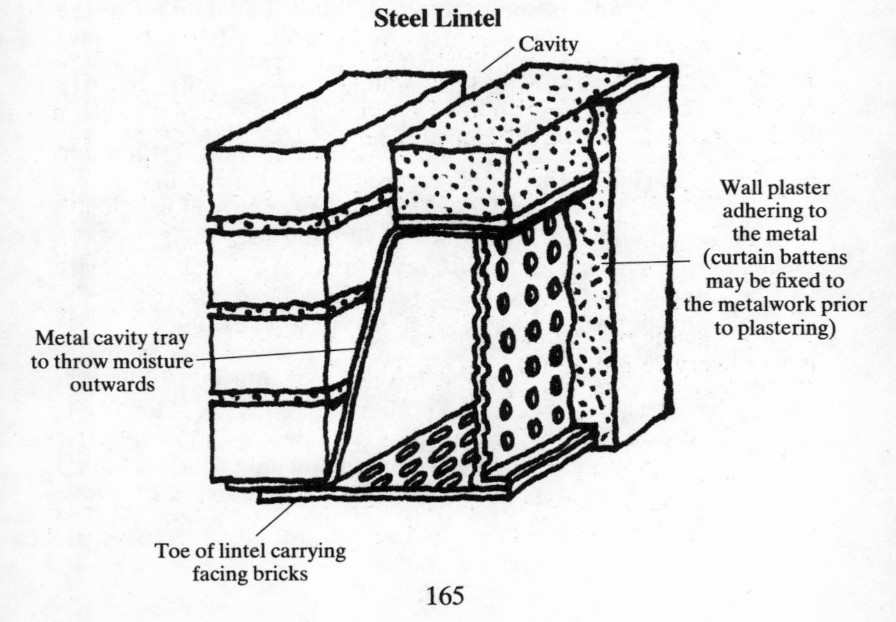

Concrete Lintel

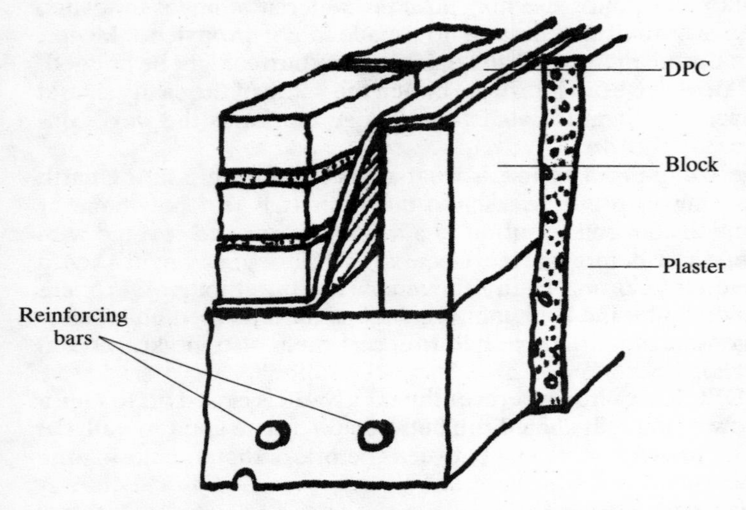

All window and door cavities will require a **lintel** over them. For some reason architects spell the word 'lintol' but they mean the same thing. At least three courses of brick must be built above concrete lintels to provide additional strength. This is not necessary with pre-formed metal lintels such as Catnics. These are lighter and some are designed to act as a lintel for both the internal and the external leaves of the cavity wall. Lintels must have a minimum overlap or **bearing** on the supporting walls of 150 mm (6 in).

Where a lintel is used the DPC will be taken over the top of it and then diagonally upwards inside the cavity and over the top of the blocks inside, thus ensuring that any drips that get into the cavity will be directed down and outwards. **Weep holes** are left in the vertical joints of the brickwork to let the moisture escape.

If a new wall is being joined to an old one to create, for example, a porch or an extension, they may have to be **combed** together with old and new bricks alternating. Another method is to cut a channel into the old wall, but this can weaken it. Nowadays most builders use patent galvanized or stainless-steel **channelling** which is bolted to the old wall. The sides of the channel hold the bricks or blocks of the new wall and the back has tabs to provide an anchor for ties.

One of the problems with having an extension built is getting brick to match. In the case of fairly modern houses it is not too difficult to find an exact match within the makers' catalogues. Naturally the new bricks will not have had a chance to weather but after a few years or so it will be difficult to see the join. Older houses may present more problems with this but reclaimed brick from an architectural salvage yard may be the answer. However, be prepared to pay a lot for rarities. Coveted old bricks such as Tudor reds could cost around £600 per thousand.

Sometimes just a few bricks are needed to replace those damaged by **spalling**, crumbling due to the effect of water getting in and then expanding when it freezes. There may be a source of original bricks around the house in the form of an obsolete coal bunker or a support wall for an already dilapidated greenhouse. The builders may have just left odd bricks lying around the garden or under the floorboards following the construction of the sleeper walls. But if there are no secret hoards then it's back to the catalogue or the demolition yard.

Damaged bricks can be removed completely if you chisel away the pointing until a bar or chisel inserted first at one end and then at the other wiggles it free. It is then a simple job to put a thin layer of mortar around the hole, insert the replacement and repoint. Sometimes it is easier to insert a **queen**, a brick cut in half lengthways. Use a bolster chisel to cut away the damaged brick to half its width and then mortar in the queen.

Brickwork can often suffer damage at the bottom where the rain splashes up and keeps it soaked. The answer is to make an **apron** of rendering to a height of 30-50 cm (12-18 in), using a waterproofing agent in the mix.

Stonework can also suffer damage, particularly the softer sandstones and limestone. If a replacement stone is available then it is just a matter of chiselling away the mortar holding the old one. Where there is no similar stone it may be necessary to fake one with render. Chop out the damaged stone and if the hole is a large one it should be built up with expanded metal laths or just tiles sandwiched in mortar. Add a liquid or powder cement-colouring agent to a mix of 4 parts crushed stone to 1 part cement, spread a small amount on a piece of board and let it dry so you can check the colour against the wall. Keep adjusting the tone until it is satisfactory and then render the hole.

The mortar joints or **pointing** between bricks or stones can be treated in different ways for decorative effect and practical reasons:

POINTING

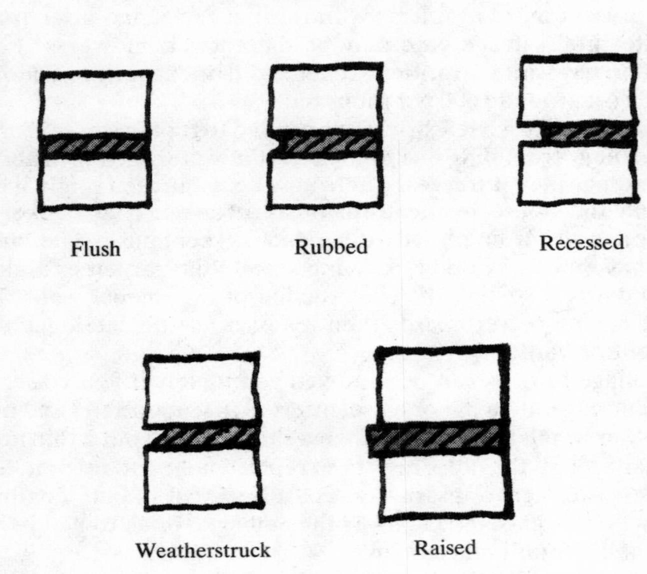

- **Flush joints** are created by the mortar being cut off vertically in a line with the bricks.
- **Rubbed joints** have an inward curve put into the mortar by a piece of pipe being run along it.
- **Recessed joints** leave the bricks standing proud of the mortar. Because this encourages the collection of water these joints should be used only in sheltered positions.
- **Weatherstruck joints** are made with a trowel used at an angle to press the mortar in at the top of the joint and allow it to overhang very slightly at the bottom. This encourages the mortar to shed water rather than to allow it to soak in.

- **Raised joints** are used only for stonework as they collect water which would damage brick. A generous amount of mortar is trowelled flat and then cut in lines using a straight-edged piece of timber and trowel or a fork with the centre prongs removed. A trowel is then used to clean up the pointing.

The trimming of mortar is often done with a **Frenchman**. You will not, however, be forced to look in the Lonely Hearts columns for such an assistant, since it's actually an old knife with the end bent at a right angle and filed to a point. It is guided along the horizontal joints by a straight-edged piece of timber which is held away from the wall by packing at each end so that the surplus mortar drops to the ground between it and the wall. Where repointing is necessary the old joints should first be chiselled out to a depth of 10 mm (½ in). Lay sacking or polythene on the ground to collect all the bits of fresh mortar that drop or are cut away. When the pointing is complete let it harden a little before using a soft brush to remove wayward crumbs of mortar.

Timber frames: Not all walls are brick or stone. Timber framing is a modern version of a technique used in medieval times. Most systems use factory-made panels which are bolted together on site, making construction very fast. A brick or stone facing skin is then usually built in front of the panel walls, although this carries no load. Timber framing is treated to make it highly fire- and rot-resistant, and the construction is heavily insulated. One snag is that a vapour barrier is incorporated into the framing, preventing moisture from making its way outside through the walls, which can lead to condensation problems. It is significant that these houses are very common in North America and Scandinavia where there is a great temperature range but fairly low humidity. The problem of condensation is overcome to some extent by the presence in the building of a fireplace and chimney to provide ventilation. Timber frames are extremely durable and a National House-Building Council inquiry into complaints about the system in Britain found that almost all problems were due to faulty workmanship.

Rendering and plastering: Internal walls can be made from brick, block or **stud** partitions of timber (see page 120). Solid walls can be plastered in the traditional way, but it is increasingly common to

dry line both them and stud walls. Plasterboard is stuck to the blocks or nailed to the timber partition and then either it is skimmed with plaster or the joints are filled and the boards decorated as they stand. Timber-framed houses are invariably dry lined and decorated. The system makes life easier for amateurs and doesn't take two months to dry out, but to the purist the finish doesn't have the appeal of plaster polished to a gleaming flat surface. Cement render is used to protect external block walls, to make old brick walls weatherproof, or just as a decorative finish.

Render: Very strong rendering mixes are liable to shrinkage and cracking so it is essential not to use too much cement. For blocks use 1 part cement to 6 parts sand, plus a plasticizer. For bricks the mix could be a little stronger.

Before work is started all loose material must be cleared from the wall, the joints chiselled out to a depth of 10 mm (½ in) and the wall painted with a bonding agent. Large areas will need **screeding battens**, measuring about 9 mm (⅜ in) by 38 mm (1½ in), which are nailed vertically to the wall about 1½ m (6 ft) apart to create a series of bays and to mark the thickness of the render. Don't bang the nails home as the boards will have to be removed later. Rendering is not a job for using ladders and scaffolding is essential if you are to be able to reach all parts of the wall.

The mortar is put on the hawk which is angled so that the float can take a lump off. Using the float, push the mortar on to the wall, working from the bottom corner of the first bay. The mortar should end up slightly higher than the screed battens and when the bay is finished a straight-edged piece of timber should be scraped across the battens to remove the surplus. Fill in any hollows and repeat until the surface is even. Boards or polythene should be placed at the bottom of the wall to collect the excess mortar which can then be used again.

When all the bays are filled leave the mortar for a few hours until it has started to go off, remove the battens and fill, and scratch the surface to provide a key for a second coat. One coat of rendering might be enough but two is better. The second coat should be thinner and trowelled smooth if a **stucco** finish is required. Do not overdo the trowelling, though, or the cement will be brought to the surface and will crack and dust up as it dries.

A wooden float will give a slightly rougher, matt finish, or the render can be deliberately **textured** with special combs or balls of newspaper or anything that comes to hand. A **Tyrolean** finish is a rough finish produced by machine that hurls the render on when a handle is turned. **Roughcast** has fine shingle mixed in the wet mortar and **pebbledash** has flint chippings thrown by hand on to the wet mortar.

To repair a rendered wall use a club hammer and a chisel to remove any loose render and rake out the joints in the brickwork. Paint on the bonding agent and apply the mortar with the float. Using a board held edge-on, saw across the new render to bring it flush with the old, and finish the surface to match.

Plaster: Plastering needs a similar technique to rendering. Again, brush down the wall and nail 9-mm (⅜-in) thick screeding battens to it if necessary. Corners need to have expanded metal **beads** attached to reinforce the plaster and to provide a guide for the plasterer to get a neat edge. Add the plaster slowly to the water, not the other way round. The mixed plaster should be thick enough not to fall off the mixing stick but not so solid that it won't tip out of the bucket.

Damp the wall, put plaster on the hawk, transfer it to the float and push the plaster on to the wall, holding the float at an angle to it so that a slight bow wave is created. Again fill the gap between the screeds and then work the straight-edged timber upwards to remove the surplus. Fill the hollows and repeat. When the plaster has gone off a little the screeds can be removed and filled.

If one-coat plaster is being used, the surface should be smoothed and polished with a clean damp steel float and a damp sponge. Attack it at intervals as it hardens to try and get that glass-like finish that is the mark of a professional.

If a finishing coat is to be applied, roughen the surface with the edge of the float and apply a 3-mm (⅛-in) thick coat. Then polish with the float.

Few amateurs will ever achieve a perfectly flat plastered wall, and ceilings represent an even greater challenge. As a result it is best to leave the ceiling alone until at least some measure of competence has been gained or you are liable to end up a demoralized, plaster-covered wreck with aching arms and back. The technique is the same as for the walls but a platform of planks will have to be built to work off.

FLOORS

A base for a new concrete floor is provided by hard core such as broken stone and brick consolidated by rolling or ramming down.

To prevent damp from rising through a concrete raft or solid floor a damp-proof membrane of thick polythene is laid over the hard core, which should first be **blinded** with a layer of sand to avoid punctures. Solid floors should have a 150-mm (6-in) thickness of concrete. On top of this will go a 75-mm (3-in) smooth **screed** and then the final surface, such as tiles. To improve insulation and to create a softer surface for the feet a **floating floor** of chipboard is sometimes laid on a frame over the concrete. Solid floors can also be made up of prefabricated slabs which rest on a beam, and the slabs often have insulation material built in underneath them.

If the floor is suspended it is vital to build air-bricks into the wall that will provide the timber with ventilation. The joists will be either inserted into the internal block walls, rest on a timber **wallplate** attached to the wall or supported on galvanized metal **hangers**. Where joists meet, hangers are also used to connect them together. **Sleeper walls** provide support for joists in the middle of rooms and these walls too must have an open section or air-bricks in to ensure ventilation. Joists must be kept at least 38 mm (1½ in) away from chimney breasts and they will be **trimmed** round with a support joist rather than be set in the breast. When the ends of joists were always set into walls it did help to prevent them from twisting. This is now done by **strutting** with pieces of wood or patent metal struts which are fixed in a diagonal or herring-bone pattern between the joists. The floor **decking** can be tongue-and-grooved hardwood or softwood boards, chipboard or plywood. Where ply or chipboard is being used, care must be taken to make sure that the spacing of the joists matches the dimensions of the sheets. If the ceiling joists are at 450-mm (18-in) centres 9-mm (⅜-in) thick plasterboard can be used, but if the gap is larger than that the boards will have to be 13 mm (½ in) thick.

THE ROOF

When the walls reach roof height the cavity is closed and a wallplate fixed to the top. This will support the rafters which should be notched over it in a **bird's-mouth** joint. As we said earlier, the rafters meet at the top of the roof at the ridge board and they are supported half-way down by the purlins. At the bottom the rafters are tied by the ceiling joists and these are supported in the middle of the house by a load-bearing wall. **Struts** may go from this wall to the purlins at the rate of one every fourth rafter and each joist may be further supported by a **hanger**, a vertical piece of timber attached to a rafter. This complicated but strong construction method is being usurped by **truss rafters** which need no support from an internal wall and are quick to assemble. Because they are very light, the wallplate must be fixed to the wall with galvanized metal straps to avoid the whole structure being blown away in a gale. Each rafter is nailed to the wallplate, and the whole system is supported with **wind braces** running diagonally from the top corner to the bottom one. At the ridge a **longitudinal brace** is attached to hold the rafters the correct distance apart.

SECTION THROUGH EAVES

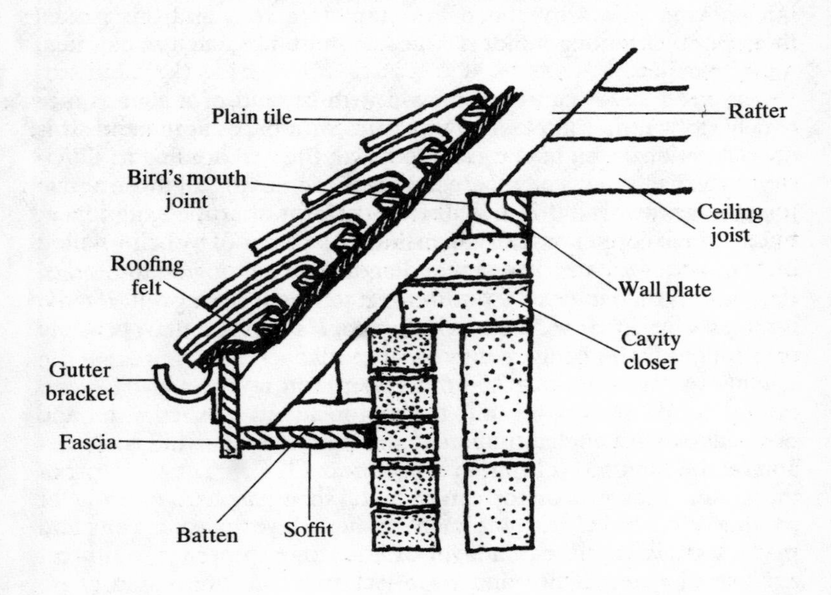

The roof is covered with rolls of felt. Start at the eaves and work up the roof making sure each layer overlaps the one below by at least 150 mm (6 in). The battens which will take the tiles or slates are nailed over this. The more gentle the pitch of the roof the more slowly the water runs off, so the better the final weatherproofing has to be.

Slates can be used on a roof with an angle as low as 30° because they are all nailed to the battens. They may be **head nailed** with two nails at the top or **centre nailed** with two in the middle. With the first row along the eaves, the slates are laid side by side and overlapped at the head to hide the nails.

Tiles are nailed only every third or fourth course as a precaution against the wind getting under and lifting them off. Instead they rely on their **nibs** or little projections to hold them. As a result a steeper pitch to the roof of 35-40° is needed. **Plain** tiles half overlap the row below, while **interlocking** tiles link along their edges. Fewer interlocking tiles are needed to complete a roof and this makes them popular among builders. Tiles without nibs, such as pantiles, must be nailed.

Damaged slates can be removed with the aid of a **slate ripper** which looks rather like a long flat knife with barbs at the end. It is passed under the slate and used to break the nail holding it. Obviously you can't nail a new slate in without removing all those above it so the answer is a **tingle**. This is not a form of erotic experience, but a strip of copper or lead which is fixed to the roof by being nailed or bent under a slate. The new slate is placed on top and the end of the tingle is bent under the bottom of it to stop it sliding out. If a tile is nailed, the ripper will be needed again. If not it is usually possible to get it out by levering up the row above it.

Flat roofs need joists at 450-mm (18-in) centres from wall to wall. A slight slope must be given to the roof to allow it to shed water and this is done with angled timbers or **firring pieces**. The fall is at least 1 in 60, i.e. 5 mm (3⁄16 in) in every 300 mm (12 in). The waterproof membrane that goes on top can be metal sheet, asphalt, multi-layer roofing felt bonded with bitumen or single-layer plastic. Felts and plastics are covered with a layer of fine stone chippings to protect against an external fire and to reflect sunshine that could cause cracking.

INDEX

Note: page numbers in italic refer to illustrations

INDEX